Squeaking Wheels
Of Comans Well, Sussex, Virginia

Hugh Mayes

2020

Trilogy Christian Publishers

A Wholly Owned Subsidary of Trinity Broadcasting Network

2442 Michelle Drive

Tustin, CA 92780

For information, address Trilogy Christian Publishing

Rights Department, 2442 Michelle Drive, Tustin, Ca 92780.

Trilogy Christian Publishing/ TBN and colophon are trademarks of Trinity Broadcasting Network.

For information about special discounts for bulk purchases, please contact Trilogy Christian Publishing.

Manufactured in the United States of America

Trilogy Disclaimer: The views and content expressed in this book are those of the author and may not necessarily reflect the views and doctrine of Trilogy Christian Publishing or the Trinity Broadcasting Network.

10 9 8 7 6 5 4 3 2 1

Library of Congress Cataloging-in-Publication Data is available.

B-ISBN#: 978-1-64773-560-9

E-ISBN#: 978-1-64773-561-6

Dedication

I am blessed and have been by many people in my life; my deceased parents, siblings, wife, extended family members, neighbors, Sunday School teachers, preachers, teachers, professors, doctors, friends, and churches. There are two people through God's leadership that truly adjusted the course of my life. I was a Christian at the time. I felt called to the ministry as a pastor. I had no resources or direction on how to accomplish the task. In my teenage years, I would watch Gospel Music on TV before going to church. I had never been to a gospel singing other than local preachers or local church choirs. I felt called to preach at the age of sixteen.

Musically I was a fan of rock and country music. Pauline and John Kennedy invited a gospel group to our church. I went to support the Kennedys and our church. We were a small church, and I hated for no one to be there. I was surprised to see the church packed. I had to sit in the balcony. That night God adjusted my course. God began healing a depressed young man through the ministry of gospel music.

I bought albums as I left that night. I started listening to Claude and Connie instead of Sonny and Cher. The "Hopper Brothers and Connie" were my favorite group on the TV programs on Sunday morning when I was a teenager. I do not remember their name, but I remembered that the brothers sang, and a lady sang and played the piano. Not only did they minister through the music, but they financially helped me through college and seminary. They became true friends.

I dedicate this book to Claude and Connie Hopper and thank you and God for changing the course of my life.

Table of Contents

Foreword

I have always heard that the squeaking wheel is the one that gets oiled. Our lives are full of ups and downs that evaluate too many squeaks that need oil. We need God's healing power and guidance for whatever squeaks we face in life. Through our faith in Jesus as our Lord and Savior and the power of the Holy Spirit, we are oiled. Praise God for His divine touch, guidance, healing, and oiling of our lives.

The people mentioned in this book did not all live in Comans Well, Sussex, Virginia but have affected the lives of someone who has lived in Comans Well. I am the longest living resident of Comans Well. I am a squeaking wheel of Comans Well, Sussex, Virginia, who has been oiled by God's grace, mercy, and healing power.

I thank Gary M. Williams for his help in recalling the history of Comans Well. I grew up with an oral tradition of the history of Comans Well. Through the reading of his book *Sussex County, Virginia: A Heritage Recalled By the Land,* I have been able to put dates and events in order. Gary happened to come into the Sussex, Virginia Post Office when I was mailing the first rough draft of this book to the Hoppers. He said I could use his book as a source and asked for a copy of the rough draft to read. Gary has been the Clerk of the Circuit Court since 1976. The records of Sussex County have been in good hands. I have been in and out of the office researching for the book. I am amazed at his skill in researching the records to reveal the history of our county.

When I was ordained as a Baptist Minister in 1979, I was in no hurry to get my license to perform weddings. A couple came up and wanted to get married right away. I came to the clerk's office, and Gary handled it in time for me to perform the wedding.

Chapter 1

Influences Before Establishment

In the beginning God created the heaven and the earth.

(Genesis 1:1 KJV)

So God created man in his own image, in the image of God created he him; male and female created he them.

(Genesis 1:27 KJV)

Therefore shall a man leave his father and his mother, and shall cleave unto his wife: and they shall be one flesh.

(Genesis 2:24 KJV)

Let us hear the conclusion of the whole matter: Fear God and keep his commandments: for this is the whole duty of man. For God shall bring every work into judgment, with every secret thing, whether it be good, or whether it be evil.

(Ecclesiastes 12:13–14 KJV)

In the beginning was the Word, and the Word was with God, and the Word was God.

(John 1:1 KJV)

For God so loved the world that he gave his only begotten Son, that whosoever believeth in him should not perish, but have everlasting life.

(John 3:16 KJV)

For all have sinned, and come short of the glory of God; Being justified freely by his grace through the redemption that is in Christ Jesus:

(Romans 3:23–24 KJV)

Behold, I stand at the door, and knock: if any man hear my voice, and open the door, I will come in to him, and will sup with him, and he with me.

(Revelation 3:20 KJV)

And God shall wipe away all tears from their eyes; and there shall be no more death, neither sorrow, nor crying, neither shall there be any more pain: for the former things are passed away.

(Revelation 21:4 KJV)

Chapter 2

Early Family History

Our family tree starts with William Robinson (1785–1854), who descended from John Robinson of the Mayflower. William Robinson had a son Robert. Robert had a daughter Mollie Robinson. Mollie married Emmett Lewis; they are my great-grandparents.

John Robinson (1576–1625) was the pastor of the "Pilgrim Fathers" before they left on the *Mayflower*. He became one of the early leaders of the English Separatists and is regarded (along with Robert Browne) as one of the founders of the Congregational Church. Robinson was born at Sturton-Le-Steeple in Nottinghamshire, England. He was educated at Queen Elizabeth's Grammar School, Gainsborough, Lincolnshire, and entered Corpus Christi College at the University of Cambridge in April 1592. He received his Bachelor of Arts degree in 1596. In May 1598, he was admitted a Fellow of his college and ordained a priest of the Church of England. This was followed one year later in 1599 by his Master of Arts degree. Following the attainment of his master's degree, he obtained two positions at Corpus: *Praelector Graecus*, a lectureship in Greek, and *Decanus*, a post involving student oversight.

Cambridge was the center of Puritanism. During his years there, Robinson gradually accepted its principles. The leaders of this movement strongly criticized the English Church because they believed its beliefs and rituals were too much like those of the Roman Catholic Church. The reforms they advocated would "purify" the established church from within; for this reason, they became known as "Puritans".

When James I succeeded Elizabeth I in 1603, he instituted a policy designed to enforce religious conformity. The Puritans would, he warned, adhere or he would "harry them out of the land."[1] James

---

[1] "John Robinson (Pastor)." 2020. Wikipedia, The Free Encyclopedia. 2020. https://en.wikipedia.org/wiki/John_Robinson_(pastor).

I enforced the 1593 Act Against Puritans, which made it illegal for them to hold their own separate services. Those who refused to attend the Church of England for forty days were imprisoned without bail until they agreed to yield and conform to the Church of England. [2]In August 1603, Robinson became associate pastor of St. Andrew's Church in the commercial center of Norwich. The city had contacts on the continent with Holland and Flanders. Soon after he assumed his duties in St. Andrews, James 1 issued a proclamation requiring to conform to a new book of canons. The deadline to conform was set for the end of November. Robinson left the church.

College fellows were prohibited from marrying, so Robinson resigned his fellowship to wed Bridget White, on 15 February 1604 at St. Mary's Church, Greasley in western Nottinghamshire.[3]

About 1607, John joined the Separatists who met in the home of William Brewster, the local postmaster, and bailiff at his home, Scrooby Manor. Richard Clyfton became the pastor, John was the assistant pastor, William Bradford was soon joined the congregation, and they became known as the "pilgrims and strangers upon the earth." This congregation secretly walked sixty miles with their possessions to the seaport of Boston in Lincolnshire, where a sea captain agreed to smuggle them to the Netherlands. Before they arrived, the captain betrayed them to the authorities, who took all their money, ransacked their baggage, put them on public display, and confined them in cells in the Boston Guildhall. They were imprisoned for a month and treated well, although Richard Clyfton, John Robinson, and William Brewster were the last to be released. The second attempt to flee was successful, and Clyfton, Robinson, and Brewster followed last to help the weakest for the journey. The first settlement was Amsterdam; their

---

[2] Rev John Robinson Jr. (1576–1625) Find A Grave Memorial:1." 2002. Find A Grave Memorial. 2002. https://www.findagrave.com/memorial/6238808/john-robinson.

[3] "John Robinson (Pastor)." 2020.

congregation became known as the "Ancient Church".[4]

For two years with John Robinson, the minister to the Pilgrims in England and later in Holland, John Smyth helped organize Separatist in Nottinghamshire. In 1608 both Smyth and Robinson went with their followers to Amsterdam. Adopting Baptist principles there, Smyth baptized first himself and then others.[5]

In February 1609, Robinson and about 100 followers petitioned the City of Leiden for permission to resettle there by May 1, 1609. Soon after the congregation resettled in Leiden, John Robinson became the Leiden Separatist's sole pastor. The congregation came to number several hundred.

John Robinson was instrumental in the arrangements for the Mayflower. Since a majority of the church remained behind in Leiden, he made the very difficult decision to stay and minister to those remaining in Holland rather than come on the Mayflower. He planned to come to America as soon as he could get more of his church over, but his untimely death prevented his ever making it to the New World.[6]

"The Lord has more truth yet to break forth out of His Holy Word," John Robinson said to the Pilgrims as they set sail for America. [7]William Bradford's book Of Plymouth Plantation, 1620–1647, has many references to John Robinson. My favorite is in a letter dated December 19, 1623. "Concerning the killing of those poor Indians, of which we heard at first by report, and since by more certain relation. Oh, how happy a thing had it been if you had converted some before you had killed any! Besides, where blood is once begun to be shed, it is seldom staunched of a long time after."[8]

[4] "Rev John Robinson Jr. (1576–1625) Find A Grave Memorial:2." 2002.
[5] "John Smyth: English Minister." 2020. In Encyclopedia Britannica. Encyclopedia Britannica, inc. https://www.britannica.com/biography/John-Smyth.
[6] "John Robinson (Pastor)." 2020.
[7] Dowely, Tim. 1978. Eerdmans' Handbook to the History of Christianity. Hertz, England: Lion Publishing.
[8] Bradford, William. 1997. Of Plymouth Plantation 1620–1647. New York, NY:

Despite his plans to sail to the Americas, John became ill on Saturday 22nd of 1625, and while he recovered long enough to preach twice the next day, he died the following Sunday, March 1, 1625, interred at St Peter's on the fourth of March. He was fifty years old.[9]

John Robinson's son, Isaac Robinson, came to Plymouth Colony in 1631.[10]

Isaac Robinson (1704-1766), my fifth great-grandfather, was born in Sussex, Virginia.[11] He obtained a land patent or grant.[12] His son Isaac was born in 1744 and died in 1807. Isaac's son William was born in 1785 and died in 1854. William is my third great-grandfather.[13] Isaac, my fourth great-grandfather, was an elder. According to The Concise History of the Kehukee Association, two elders, John Rivers and Isaac Robinson, desired to have a Baptist Church in their neighborhood.[14] A building was constructed near Sappony Creek, approximately three miles from what is now the present-day town of Stony Creek. This building would be known as the Sappony Meeting House. The origin of the name comes from the Sappony Indian tribe who lived in the area. The building was built in 1773.[15] I was licensed to preach by Sappony Baptist Church on its 205th Homecoming on June 4, 1978. I was ordained to preach by Sappony Baptist Church on May 27, 1979.

Alfred A. Knopf.

[9] "Rev John Robinson Jr. (157–1625) Find A Grave Memorial:3." 2002.

[10] "Isaac Robinson (1610–1704)." 2009. Find A Grave Memorial. 2009. https://www.findagrave.com/memorial/34758126/isaac-robinson.

[11] "Isaac Robinson 1744–1807." 2020. Ancestry.Com. 2020. Ancestry.com/family-tree/person/tree/159990938person/382092415489/story.

[12] Williams, Gary Murdock. 2012. *Sussex County, Virginia: A Heritage Recalled by the Land.* The Dietz Press. 365 (321).

[13] "William Robinson 1785–1854." 2020. Ancestry.Com. 2020. Ancestry.com/family-tree/person/tree/1609777755/person/392116031581/facts.

[14] "Sappony Baptist Church." n.d. Sappony Baptist Church. Accessed September 13, 2020. https://www.sappony1773.org/.

[15] Ibid

Chapter 3

The Early Days of Comans Well, Sussex, Virginia

In 1988, an extraordinary discovery was made after Harold Conover, a Dinwiddie county farmer, who dabbled in Indian archaeology, noticed some arrowheads in recently dropped road fill near him. His curiosity in determining the source where these artifacts had been transported led him to the banks of the Nottoway River in Sussex, on the west side of what is now known as Railroad Bed Road, where the landowner, Union Camp Corporation, had been selling its sand for fill dirt. Conover called on fellow archaeologist, Joseph McAvoy, to make an investigation. McAvoy had further contact with Russell Darden, an employee of Union Camp and longtime archaeological enthusiast, who assisted in halting the commercial activity. A serious dig ensured for several years, and the results of that survey made national headlines.

This is the investigation known as the Cactus Hill survey (the site fell on Robert Hawthorne's 1701 patent of 1,400 acres along the banks of the river). Named by McAvoy for the numerous cactus plants growing along the rim of a sandy hill, it was acknowledged as "the oldest site of human habitation yet found in this hemisphere."[16] Harold Conover is a friend, and I performed his wedding with Mary Dunn Lilley.

If Sussex County can claim, at least for a while, to have harbored the very first Americans. Its human history must remain very much in the dark for the broad sweep of thousands of intervening centuries before the English arrived. How long the Nottoway Indians or, as they called themselves, the Cheroenhakas were there before 1607 is unknown. But these peaceful red people who lived and hunted along the Nottoway, leaving behind millions of spear points for collectors to

---

[16] Williams, Gary Murdock. 2012, 2.

find, are really the first citizens to whom we can relate. This land, once so beautiful with its virgin forests and clear waters, was their domain, and while their Cactus Hill predecessors have attracted the scrutiny of many scholars far beyond our borders, our concern will be on the inhabitants who made the immediate link to the world we now know.

The Nottoways were not part of the great Powhatan Confederacy, who interacted most frequently with the Jamestown colonists. The Nottoways were Iroquois, and their kinsmen were the Cherokees and the Tuckaroras of North Carolina and the Meherrins of the Virginia Piedmont.[17] My wife Carol has Cherokee relatives.

Between 1671 and 1772, the Sappony and Tutelo moved away from the Virginia foothills to avoid the Iroquoian enemy attacks. They settled with the Occaneechi on islands at the junction of the Staunton and Dan Rivers, near present-day Clarksville, Virginia. This island location allowed the Indians to benefit from trade between the English settlers and other Indian tribes to the west.

In 1676 these Indians became involved in Bacon's Rebellion, a war that began with conflicts between the English and the Iroquoian Susquehannocks. The English and several Indian tribes friendly to the colonists, including the Sappony, signed a treaty at the end of the war. *The Treaty of Middle Plantation* changed the relationship of the Sappony and their allies with King Charles of Great Britain and with the English colonials. Now the government recognized the Sappony as a "tributary tribe," meaning they agreed to maintain peace with the colonists and pay a yearly tribute in fur and skins. For this, they were guaranteed homeland and protection by the Colonial government.[18]

Carol and I have been to powwows of the Nottoway tribe and the Sappony tribe. Daddy has picked up many arrowheads by the banks of the Nottoway River while plowing in my uncles' fields.

---

[17] Williams, Gary Murdock. 2012, 4.
[18] "Sappony Indians." n.d. NCPedia: State Library of NC. 2020. https://www.ncpedia.org/sappony-indians.

The land comprising Sussex County remained the domain of Native Americans until 1693 when 10,000 acres on Joseph and Coppahaunk Swamp were granted in chartering the College of William and Mary. While this land initially was only to be leased to the English settlers, rather than sold, to support the college, the balance of that portion of Surry County south of the Blackwater River was also made available for legal settlements. Settlers could apply for patents or land grants through the office of the Secretary of the Colony, which were signed by the acting royal governor in the name of the king or queen, and the beginnings of individual land ownership in what became Sussex County ensured.[19] Comans Well is located on Allen's Road on grants to Robert Jones Jr. and the Graves family.[20] Today, Comans Well address is Comans Well Road, Yale, Virginia.

The house that is the centerpiece for the village sharing its name was built by William H. Comann in 1825. The hostelry (offering twenty-two beds, as listed by Comann) was a stagecoach stop for travelers on what was then Allen's Road, the essential east-west route across the county. The mineral water from the well, an added feature, was desired for its medicinal qualities. Comann lost the place by financial reversals in 1829, but he and his wife Leonora were permitted to live there for many years.[21] William H. Comann was a Methodist minister. Comann Well was a healing spa.[22] In 1827, there is a transfer of one hundred acres known as Comann's Well "except one acre to be laid off square for the meeting house called Fredonia."[23] William H. Comann was apparently the founder of this Church (c. 1828). His

---

[19] Williams, Gary Murdock. 2012, 313.
[20] Ibid, Map 16, 330.
[21] Williams, Gary Murdock. 2012, 100.
[22] "William H Coleman." 2020. Ancestry.Com. 2020. William H Coleman,ancestry.com%0Aancestry.com/familytree/78467263/person/3639059364/facts?phsrc=mmh640&phstaet=successSource%0A.
[23] Williams, Gary Murdock. 2012

heirs had it sold in 1856.[24] William H. Comann died in 1850.[25]

The north side of Allen's Road was the Grave's family land grant. There were three plantation homes built upon the land grant by members of the Grave's family. They were Cedar Springs, Cedar Level, and Elm Shade. The preliminary map of a part of south of the James River from surveys and reconnaissances made under the direction of Maj. A. H. Campbell P. E. in ch'ge Top' Dept. D.N.V. December 1864 shows four dots on the south side of Allen's Road and three dots on the north side of Allen's Road. On the south side of the road were Bonnie Doon, Methodist parsonage, Comann house, and Fredonia Church. On the north side were Sharon Church, the store, and a house. I do not have a record of the house, but Daddy remembers a house being there. Daffodils bloomed every year on the lot beside my house where this house was until in the 1990s when someone came and dug them up.

Albemarle Parish, soon after its creation, was the recipient of a silver communion service donated under the will of John Allen of Claremont, Surry County, who died in 1741. The silver, made in London around 1747, continued in use long after disestablishment. The Diocese of Virginia reported the silver communion service was kept by Emmanuel Episcopal Church, consecrated in 1846.[26] According to https://www.familysearch.org/wiki/en/Sussex_County,_Virginia_Genealogy, Albemarle Parish was a pre-revolutionary war Episcopal parish that reflected the political and civil dominance of the Church of England in the affairs of Virginia at the time.[27] Albemarle Parish should not be confused with Albemarle County. Sussex County was formed in 1754 (some sources say 1753) from the part of Surry County that was south of the Blackwater River.

---

24 Ibid.
25 "William H Coleman." 2020.
26 Williams, Gary Murdock. 2012, 48.
27 Ibid.

The new county of Sussex was in Albemarle Parish. In fact, all of Albemarle Parish was then located in Sussex County. The church was across from Cedar Level. There is a record of four churches within a mile and a half of Comans Well; not all were open at the same time.

In 1835, William Taylor purchased the Comann house.[28] A post office was established there in 1827, then a general store under the name of William D. Taylor and Company, followed by a girls' school. By 1836, the village had gained a blacksmith's shop and a tailor's shop.[29] I have a ledger from William D. Taylor and Company; the earliest entry is on September 28, 1836, and the last entry was on September 18, 1840. William D. Taylor was appointed postmaster on January 5, 1832. William D. Taylor Jr. was appointed postmaster on July 9, 1857.[30]

At Comans Well, William D. Taylor's School for Young Ladies was flourishing in the 1830s. Little boys in the neighborhood were among the pupils. In charge of this academy was Mrs. Anna Durant Taylor, who was aided by a staff of four women.[31]

A parsonage for the minister serving nearby Methodist churches was built in 1840. Bonnie Doon, built in 1826 at Comans Well, was the residence of two doctors, Dr. Richard H. Ramsey (the Scotsman who built it) and Dr. William Lewis, who died there in 1831.[32]

In 1807, a two-acre tract of land, about three miles south of Sussex Courthouse, was deeded to the following five trustees: William Graves, James Rogers, Maurice Pennington, John Pennington, and Fred Pennington. On this tract Providence Methodist Episcopal Church was built. Nothing is known of the early history of this church.

---

[28] Ibid, 100.

[29] Ibid, 102.

[30] "U.S., Appointments of U. S. Postmasters, 1832–1971." 2020. Ancestry.Com. 2020. https://www.ancestry.com/search/collections/1932/.

[31] Writers' Program (U.S.). Virginia, Virginia Writers' Project. 1942. Sussex County: A Tale of Three Centuries. Whittet & Shepperson. 324 (32).

[32] Williams, Gary Murdock. 2012, 102.

In 1844, a tract of land, in the village of Comans Well, was given, on which Sharon Methodist Protestant Church was built in 1846. The deed giving the land "for and in consideration of the Love of God and for the *benefit* of the 'Methodist Protestant Church' (...) for the purpose of building a Methodist Protestant House of worship" was signed, sealed, and delivered by Joseph Graves on March 1, 1844 (Joseph Graves is the great-grandfather of Lynwood D. Bobbitt.) The trustees are listed as John G. Adkins, Henry Moore, John Moore, William Hartley, and John H. Marable. The year 1850 has been accepted as the year of dedication.[33]

---

[33] "Sussex Charge–Petersburg District, Virginia Conference, Sharon United Methodist Church 1850–1975." n.d.

Chapter 4

The Civil War Had a Great Impact on Southside Virginia

About four o'clock in the afternoon on May 7, 1864, the 59th Virginia Infantry C.S.A. was forced to surrender the railroad bridge over Stony Creek. There three freight cars loaded with lumber were destroyed along with wood sheds and water tanks at the depot, but the federal troops found enough corn and bacon for their whole regiment, and there they bivouacked for the night.[34]

On May 8 at Jarratt's, five Union soldiers were killed in three efforts made to reach the depot by advancing south on the Halifax Road, until they found a detour using Allen's Road and took the depot from the west. The soldiers were buried at High Hills Baptist Church in unmarked graves. The church, too, was burned by Colonel Spear's troops, as well as every dwelling in sight of the depot.

As the day unfolded on May 8, 1864, the "Battle of the White Bridge," as local residents were to call it ensured. Colonel Spears had received orders that morning from General Kautz to move north to assist in taking the bridge over the Nottoway, the longest and the highest on the railroad. Under heavy fire, the bridge, 210 feet long, caught on fire, and its remnants fell into the river in twenty minutes. Fort Nottoway, however, remained for that time impregnable, but the Yankees were satisfied they had cut a vital link in what was perhaps the Confederacy's most important railroad.[35]

The Battle of Sappony Church was a glorious Confederate victory. On June 28, 1864, the battle took place.[36] According to The *History of Virginia Portsmouth Baptist Association,* the Union soldiers under the command of General J. H. Wilson encountered Confederate soldiers under the command of General Wade

---

[34] Williams, Gary Murdock. 2012, 140.

[35] Ibid, 141.

[36] Williams, Gary Murdock. 2012, 145.

Hampton and proceeded to drive them back to Sappony Church, around which both forces skirmished during the night.[37] At the break of dawn, General Hampton's whole command charged and successfully drove the Union soldiers from two lines. Then they pursued the scattering Union forces for some two miles and captured 800 prisoners. The church was badly marred by shot and shell, the columns badly burned and torn, and the Bible was pierced. Cannon holes are still visible today above the church columns are preserved under plexiglass. The Bible was originally presented to the church in 1850 by fourteen ladies who worked together and donated twenty-five cents each to make the purchase.[38]

Despite this Confederate victory, the object of the Federal expedition south had been, in the main, accomplished. "Every railroad station, depot, water-tank, woodpile, bridge, trestle-work, tool-house, and sawmill from fifteen miles of Petersburg to the Roanoke River," wrote Brigadier General J. H. Wilson, "had been burned."[39]

The Battle of the Crater at Petersburg on July 30 was also a major Union fiasco. The Union army attempted to break through the Confederate lines, thereby exploding four tons of gunpowder in a tunnel dug beneath the Confederate fortifications. It took a heavy toll in lives on both sides, but the Confederates under General Mahone staged a successful counterattack. The explosion occurred at 4:45 a.m. by 1:00 p.m. The line had been mended. But over 4,400 men died. Every Sussex unit in the Confederate army, with the exception of the Sussex Light Dragoons, was there on that tragic day. Matthew M. Green of Comans Well was killed. Matthew was a member of the 61st Virginia.[40] Matthew had married Anna H. Taylor, the daughter

---

[37] "Sappony Baptist Church." n.d.

[38] Ibid.

[39] Writers' Program (U.S.). Virginia, Virginia Writers' Project. 1942, 87.

[40] Williams, Gary Murdock. 2012, 146.

of William D. Taylor, on May 27, 1861. He is buried in the cemetery behind the Taylor house in Comans Well, Virginia.[41]

Efforts to take the Weldon Railroad continued unabated, and by August 1864, the Union forces had the railroad line coming into Petersburg enough under their control to make Stony Creek Depot the farthest point north for railway transport. It became necessary for the rebels to transport supplies from there along Flatfoot Road, moving cargo ultimately to the Boydton Plank Road in Dinwiddie, from whence shipments would directly be sent to Lee's army.

On September 14, 1864, General Hampton led about 3,000 cavalrymen out of Dinwiddie towards Prince George County, where it had been observed that well over 2,500 cattle were grazing on what had been Edmund Ruffin's plantation on the James River, which were desperately needed to feed the soldiers of Lee's army. This engagement was what will always be remembered as the "Beefsteak Raid". These cattle were successfully captured and brought through Sussex county.[42] On September 19, they were paraded through the streets of Petersburg, along with their Confederate captors, in a jubilant celebration of what President Lincoln remarked was the "slickest piece of cattle stealing I ever heard of."[43] For Lee's half-starved army in trenches from Petersburg to Richmond, the beef was truly like manna from heaven.[44]

As the winter of 1864–65 approached, Stony Creek became the scene of much martial activity under the stimulus of a forage depot established there by Lee's cavalry. Moreover, having become a railroad terminal, it served the Confederates as a supply base for the necessary provisions carted to Petersburg after the loss of the railroad north of Reams Station. On December 1, 1864, Federal cavalry

---

[41] Ibid, 149.
[42] Ibid, 147.
[43] Williams, Gary Murdock. 2012, 149.
[44] Ibid.

raided the Stony Creek depot and captured the station guard of 170 men, eight wagons, and thirty mules, and as Brigadier General D. M. Gregg was pleased to recount, "burnt the depot" and "all shops and public buildings" and seized "about 3,000 sacks of corn, 500 bales hay, a train of cars, large quantity of bacon, government clothing, ammunition, and other stores. A few days later, on December 8th, the same cavalry was included in a force of over 30,000 men under General G. K. Warren, which tore up track, destroyed the bridge over the Nottoway River nearby, and advanced on Belfield, which was reached on December 10th.[45]

In the month of December 1864, Sussex County would experience the most devastating horrors of war, as the Union army resolved to destroy the Weldon Railroad for once and for all. On the morning of Wednesday, December 7, 1884, General Grant sent General Gouverneur K. Warren and the Fifth Corps of the U.S. Army to cripple the Weldon. Over 26,000 men were a part of this expedition. On December 8, 1864, the invading troops marched through the village of Comans Well to reach the Halifax Road at Parham's Store. Just beyond stood the rebuilt railroad bridge over the Nottoway. The Union army proceeded to burn the new bridge. The Union forces wasted no time in going about their mission and began tearing up the railroad from the Nottoway to the Meherrin River. The ties were taken up, and the rails were then heated by substantial fires enough to curve them and make them unfit for use. Frequently as the rails became pliable, they were twisted around nearby trees and left.[46]

The reason for the destruction of much property around Sussex Courthouse was fury unleashed when the returning troops encountered nude and mutilated corpse of their comrades in plain view along the road. This had been the gristly work of the rebel

---

[45] Writers' Program (U.S.). Virginia, Virginia Writers' Project. 1942, 88.
[46] Williams, Gary Murdock. 2012, 149–150.

guerrillas, who may have desecrated the bodies of their victims after the word got around that a number of defenseless women had been raped by some of the drunken Yankee soldiers. This included "a woman far advanced in pregnancy," two other local women had been ordered by Colonel Biles of the 99th Pennsylvania Infantry and one of his officers to either submit to the men's sexual gratifications or have their home burned to the ground. Indeed, both Union and Confederate sides had reason to be outraged, but the local citizens were at the mercy of their invaders. Colonel Wainwright wrote that where destruction occurred.

> None escaped, large and small, pigsties and privies, all were burnt, with barely time allowed for the people themselves to get out, saving nothing. The Negroes fared no better than whites. Every soul was turned adrift to find shelter for the night as best they could. For this barbarism, there was no real excuse unless exasperation and the innate depravity of mankind is one. I did not see the actual firing until the last of our march, but could not hear that the officers in command of the advance did anything to stop it. So pitiable a sight as the women and children turned adrift at nightfall, and most severe night, too, I never saw before and never want to see again. If this is a raid, deliver me from going on another.[47]

While passing through Comans Well, the Union forces used the Comann-Taylor house as a hospital. There are marks on a chimney where they sharpened their knives for surgery. The Taylor's son-in-law was killed in the Battle of the Crater; now, they had the Union forces in their house.

From my driveway, looking down the road toward Cedar Level, I can see the home of Milton Dunn. Milton's house is built on the site of the 1800s home. The Union forces set fire to the house. Thankfully, a Union officer came up and ordered the fire to be put out. Raymond

---

[47] Ibid, 15–156.

and Ida Ezelle lived in the house for a while when I was a child. I visited there and saw the burnt boards.

Cedar Level is less than a mile east of Comans Well. Comans Well was built on the part of the Graves family land grant. Elizabeth Susan Derby Graves (Bettie) was at home with her children, and she and the slaves heard the Yankees coming. The slaves ran and hid. Bettie then dumped a jug of molasses under the front porch to keep the Yankees from getting it. The Yankees saw fresh dirt in the backyard where the family cemetery is now located and insisted that she had buried the family treasure there, and they were going to dig it up. She told them that there was no treasure there but her babies. So, when they threatened to burn the house down, she stood up to them and said, "Over my dead body."[48] So, they burned the slave quarters instead. They also took every scrap of food in the house and kidnapped her husband, James Robert Graves. He was a Confederate Officer and was homesick at the time. They took him down the road and figured that he was going to die anyway, threw him out. He did not die, but made it home, recovered, returned to his unit, and finished the war.[49]

The Providence Church building is said to have been burned by raiders of the Northern Army during the Civil War, after having been used by them as a hospital. The Providence congregation used the Sharon building to worship in after theirs was burned.

Then, at a meeting at Sharon, the two congregations decided to unite. It was at this time that Sharon was converted to become a Methodist Episcopal Church.[50]

Our Winfield Family Cemetery has two Confederate soldiers buried in it. They are my great-great uncles Richard M. Winfield (May 1845–June 1863) and Joseph N Winfield (March 1838–April

---

[48] Personal notes communication.
[49] "Personal Notes on Cedar Level during the Civil War by Regina Davis." n.d.
[50] "Sussex Charge–Petersburg District, Virginia Conference, Sharon United Methodist Church 1850–1975." n.d.

1913). Richard M. Winfield, who had been discharged from the 16th Infantry in September 1862 on account of his youth but who re-enlisted with Company D of the 13th Virginia Calvary in June 1863 and died within a month in an encounter at Upperville.[51] Joseph N. Winfield served in the 16th Virginia Infantry. He wore a 1795 silver dollar in his boot throughout the Civil War. He passed the silver dollar down through the family to my mother, who gave it to me.

The church that I would serve the longest, Shiloh Baptist Church in Carson, Virginia, lost its organization during the Civil War. William E. Hatcher, in an article for *The Sunday School Builder* for May 1943, describes the reorganization of Shiloh Baptist Church. While pastor of Petersburg, Virginia, I was a member of the Portsmouth Association. It was not very long after the Civil War, and many of our churches had not recovered from the wreck of the war, which so thoroughly devastated that part of Virginia.

One morning the clerk of the association was calling the roll of churches. And when he cried the name of "Shiloh," the curt old moderator said, "Don't call Shiloh. Shiloh is dead." Under a painful impulse, I sprang to my feet.

"What is that?" I asked with an excited feeling. "Shiloh dead? There is something awful contradictory in talking about the death of Shiloh. When did she die? How long was she sick? Who waited on her during her illness? Where was she buried? Have any flowers been planted around her grave? Any monument built for her?"

The moderator did not seem to be noticeably sympathetic with my interruption of the roll call and said he thought it would be very well to appoint the brother to visit the grave of the dead church.

"No, sir!" I replied hotly, "I would be afraid to go. I am somewhat superstitious and believe in ghosts, and if I were to go to the grave of a dead church, I would expect to see the dance of devils in full operation around the tomb."

---

[51] Williams, Gary Murdock. 2012, 138.

Another man arose and expressed the hope that a committee should be appointed. They appointed me, and that friend of my soul, Rev. A. E. Owen, then young, but afterward, a most distinguished minister, to visit the neighborhood and preach the doctrine of the resurrection. I had no thought as to the location of the church, was surprised to find that it was not far from Petersburg. The following summer, we determined to visit the neighborhood and sent out a notice to that effect. The reply came back that the church was utterly extinct, and the house was in ruin. Word was returned that we were coming just the same.

In good time my young friend drove me through the woods to the old church, and a great surprise awaited me. True, the building itself had a look of neglect and bore many marks of dilapidation, but the yard had been cleaned up. Ever so many lunch tables had been built beneath the trees, and the yard was dotted with groups of men who were there to attend the service. I sprang out of the buggy and walked to the side door of the house, near which a group of men was standing.

"Good Morning, gentlemen," I said, without waiting for word of greeting or introduction. "I am a minister of Jesus Christ. I hear that the church at this place is dead, and I have come to sound the trumpet of life and the resurrection. If any of you have a welcome for me, I would like to grasp your hand."

With simple but hearty cordiality, they pressed around me and introduced one another to me. As soon as the handshaking was over, I stepped up into the door.

The house was more than half full of women, and I started at once singing, "Come, Thou Fount of every blessing,"[52] to the old-time tune by Greenville. Using the first stanza as a solo—which, if not melodious, was manifestly exciting enough—I sang it as I went

---

[52] "Come, Thou Fount of Every Blessing by Robert Robinson, 1758." n.d. Hymnary. Org. 2020. https://hymnary.org/text/come_thou_fount_of_every_blessing.

from the door to the pulpit and while I was setting down my baggage and pulling off my linen duster. Before the second stanza, I invited others to join in, but there was such an eager inrush of men that the second stanza got very little beyond a solo.

Then I stopped and told them to stand up and sing the last stanza. Every last one of them seemed to know it, and the rusty old shingles on the roof fairly rattled under the power of the choral song. Good people of all names and from several neighborhoods were there. We had all-day meetings through Friday evening. I was on track with only three of the former members of the church—one was a venerable woman who was no longer able to travel, the second an epileptic, and the third had denied the faith. On Saturday, I counted those who had handed in their names for then a new organization, and they totaled fifty-six.

A little later, Mr. Owen and others went with me to constitute the church, and Shiloh lived again! The fruits of that meeting were rich to a wondrous degree. Not only did the church reorganize, but it also became strong, united, and greathearted. From it went out young men and women who became eminent in commerce, education, the learned profession, and positions of Christian leadership and service.[53]

---

[53] Hatcher, William E. 1943.

Chapter 5
Comans Well Continued to Grow

William T. Freeman was born at Comans Well, Sussex County, a few months prior to the declaration of War Between the States. He was the son of John B. Freeman, a captain in the county militia, a farmer, slave owner, and one-time member of the Virginia Legislature; and Clara Taylor Freeman, daughter of Wm. D. Taylor of Comans Wells, a merchant, farmer, and slave owner.

Comans Well was at that time the largest village in the county, consisting of the largest general store in the county, which was owned by Wm. D. Taylor; shoemaker's shop, tailor's shop, tannery, wheelwright's and blacksmith's shops, school, church, post office, and three residences—those of John B. Freeman, Wm. D. Taylor, and the Methodist parsonage. The minister who lived there served the Sussex Circuit, with nine churches, several of which were twenty miles away. The tailor shop located at Comans Well kept by Moses Vaughan, and the shoemaker shop kept by Goodman Rayford, turned out superior boots and clothing for the gentry of the county, their patrons coming from extended distances.

At sixteen years of age, William T. Freeman went to work for Hartley and Bro. at Comans Well, and at twenty years of age, went to Richmond and was connected with the firm of Shelton and Minor Co. He returned to the county two years later and established the mercantile business of "W. T. Freeman and Co" in 1882, which was incorporated in 1907 under its present name of "W. T. Freeman Co., Inc."[54] He was president of Bank of Stony Creek from 1914 until his death in 1928.[55]

---

[54] *No Publishing Information Available.* 1928. "Newspaper Clipping from the Collection of Frances Mayes," 1928.
[55] Jones, Richard L. 1994. *The History of a Community Bank: The Bank of Southside Virginia, 1905–1991.* Bank of Southside Virginia/Dietz Press. 247 (139).

William Deans Taylor died on October 18, 1871. John Binns Freeman and Clara Taylor Freeman moved into the Taylor home. They had fourteen children. William Taylor Freeman moved into the Taylor home next.[56]

In 1872 the first public school in the Courthouse District was housed in the backroom of the J. B. Freeman store. It started with nine boys and nine girls though failure to maintain a daily attendance of ten pupils caused its closure in 1878. It was reopened in 1885 and continued until 1895 when all were transferred to Yale, a few miles south.[57]

Comans Well had a Post Office inside the J. B. Freeman store. William T. Freeman was appointed U.S. Postmaster on June 19, 1893.[58]

Erastus T. Thornton purchased the Fredonia Church tract and all buildings thereon in 1872. In 1873 he purchased a two-acre lot of land being the former site of Emanuel Church.[59] He had a son born in 1878, Thomas Eldridge Thornton. Erastus T. Thornton lived in the house on the Fredonia Church tract and was appointed Postmaster of Comans Well in January 1873.[60] He sold both parcels of property in 1915.[61] Thomas Eldridge Thornton was appointed Postmaster of Sussex, Sussex, Virginia, on November 17, 1911.[62] In 1913, Thomas Eldridge Thornton opened a general merchandise store in Sussex, Sussex, Virginia. He had a son Thomas Earl Thornton on October 6, 1913. Earl was appointed Postmaster of Sussex, Sussex, Virginia, on February 11, 1936.[63] Thomas Eldridge Thornton died on November 17, 1952. His sons Earl and Robert took over running the store and

---

[56] "William H Coleman." 2020.
[57] Writers' Program (U.S.). Virginia, Virginia Writers' Project. 1942, 152.
[58] "U.S., Appointments of U. S. Postmasters, 1832–1971." 2020.
[59] Sussex County Deeds, May 1915.
[60] "U.S., Appointments of U. S. Postmasters, 1832–1971." 2020.
[61] Sussex County Deeds, May 1915.
[62] "U.S., Appointments of U. S. Postmasters, 1832–1971." 2020.
[63] Ibid.

built a new store and post office building. Robert left the business. Earl died in February 1979. Earl had two children Louise and Morgan. They have continued to run the store until the present. They celebrated 100 years of the family business in 1913. Morgan was appointed the third generation Postmaster of Sussex, Sussex, Virginia, in 1979. He is the fourth generation of postmasters. Louise just retired from teaching fifty-three years in Prince George. She taught one year at L.L. Beasley Elementary and the rest of the time at Prince George High School teaching history and government. The Thornton brothers had a sign on the wall behind the cash register that always impressed me in my growing-up years. The signed said, "Destroy your enemies by making them your friends." The Thorntons were never my enemies but have been life-long friends.

A community grew around Stony Creek depot. In 1908, by an Act of the Virginia General Assembly, Stony Creek became an unincorporated town. Seven years later, the Circuit Court of Sussex County entered an order making Stony Creek an incorporated town. Phillip Freeman was elected as the town's first mayor.[64] Phillip Freeman was the son of William Taylor Freeman. He was a lawyer. The store was moved to Stony Creek. The Taylors and Freemans moved to Stony Creek and elsewhere. At the time of W. T. Freeman's death, eight of the fourteen children of John B. Freeman were still living. A son in Richmond, Virginia, two sons in New York City, two daughters in Stony Creek, a daughter in Southampton, and a daughter in Washington, D. C.[65]

---

[64] Jones, Richard L. 1994.
[65] No Publishing Information Available. 1928.

Chapter 6

The Mayes Loaded the Wagon, Moved to Comans Well

The parsonage was apparently moved permanently to Stony Creek around 1907 or 1908.[66] William Patrick Mayes (Willie) and Willie Lewis Velvin Mayes moved to the old parsonage after the preacher moved out. Granddaddy was raised about three miles from Comans Well. He was called Willie. Grandma was raised behind Lebanon Church near Chapel Hill, Sussex County, Virginia. Their tombstones have Willie P Mayes, May 17, 1886–November 4, 1961, and Willie Velvin Mayes, April 21, 1887–February 23, 1971. They were Willie and Willie. My father called her Miss Willie.

This is a latter picture of my grandparents than when they moved to Comans Well. Daddy was a baby when they moved. Pictured they are holding my sisters Pat and Dot.

---

[66] "Sussex Charge–Petersburg District, Virginia Conference, Sharon United Methodist Church 1850–1975." n.d.

Their first son was born on January 1, 1912, Lewis Patrick Mayes, my father. Their daughter was born on December 29, 1913, Frances Inez Mayes. Their youngest son was born on July 17, 1917, Joseph Wilson Mayes.

Granddaddy was a sharecropper. He farmed with mules. The family moved from house to house in Comans Well, according to which farm he farmed. They lived over a period of time in all three houses. Daddy started plowing behind a mule as soon as he was big enough to hold the plow in the ground. Granddaddy went down into the original Comans Well and said that the bottom of the well was big enough to turn a double wagon around in.

Granddaddy was a superintendent of the Sunday School of Sharon Methodist Church. Grandma said that they would feed the preacher and his horse after services. Daddy decided he did not want to go to church one Sunday morning, and he played sick. That afternoon the cousins came over, and Daddy was suddenly well and wanted to play. Granddaddy and Grandma made him sit on the porch steps and watch the other children play because he was too sick to go to church. Daddy learned a lesson for life.

Jones Chapel was about four and a half miles from Comans Well. It was opened in 1777 and continuously operated until it was closed in 1926. Jones Chapel was one of the first seven Methodist chapels established in Virginia. It was the site of the sixteenth meeting of the Virginia Conference of The Methodist Church in April 1799. A major item in the church history was the 1787 revival when over 300 persons joined the Christian Church.[67] Daddy's memory of Jones Chapel was when he was small, and Frances was a baby, they went to Jones Chapel. The church was full, and they had to sit on the chancel rail. To Granddaddy's distress, Frances wet on him. Remember, this was years before pampers. I would like to hold a revival today when 300 people were saved!

---

[67] No Publishing Information Available. 1928.

Wilson was asthmatic. He worked at a tobacco factory that did not help his health. He died with his lungs filling with fluid on June 16, 1948. Granddaddy, Grandma, and Frances moved to Stony Creek. Granddaddy had quit farming, and he retired from working for Milton Tyus in his general store. Granddaddy had hardening of the arteries and did not recognize us in his last years. I remember we would try to say the blessing at meals so he would not realize that we were praying because if he began to pray, you thought you would never get to eat. He died on November 4, 1961.

Grandma had a stroke. After the stroke, she could not remember names. You could try to tell her the wrong name, but she always would say yes when you mentioned the right name. If you mentioned a certain name, she would always say I am supposed to be mad at them, but I don't remember why. She died on February 23, 1971. Frances, after Grandma died, eventually moved back to Comans Well to live with Mama and Daddy. She died on December 11, 1986.

Chapter 7

The Lewis Family of Huske, Sussex County, Virginia

Three of Emmett Lewis's sons lived on present-day Huske road. One of them, Hugh Garnett Lewis and Martha Eva Winfield Lewis (Pattie), are my Grandparents on the Lewis side of the family. The tombstones have on them Hugh G. Lewis, September 18, 1887–May 20, 1948, and Pattie W. Lewis, March 31, 1892–August 4, 1943.

Huske was more progressive than Comans Well in the early 1900s. Comans Well is one mile off the Yale road. Wamer, my brother, had memories of them putting my bottles down the well to keep them cool. The electric line today on Comans Well Road ends a mile past Comans Well and picks up about two miles where it comes in from the west. They did not get electricity until after I was born in 1948.

Granddaddy Lewis was a farmer. I never met my Lewis Grandparents; they died before I was born in 1948. Mama kept their memory alive. The stories that my uncles and aunts would share made you wish you could have been there. The people of the community and extended family would always tell you of the good times they had at my Grandparent's house.

My Grandparents had nine children. Hugh Wright died at birth in December 1912. They lost a daughter Dorothy Jarratt who was born February 25, 1922 and died January 13, 1923. My mother, Mildred Elaine, was born February 1, 1916. There were six more: Gordon (Ethylene Smith), Virginia (George Cox), Helen (Robert Sturdivant), Katherine (John Kneeper), Garnett (Maggie Lou Leonard), and Roy (Violet Oakley)—What a blessing having a large family is. Granddaddy and Grandma had sixteen grandchildren. I had no first cousins on the Mayes side and only one aunt. On the Lewis side, I had six aunts and uncles to support me. I had fifteen first cousins to grow up with. We have the Lewis family reunion on the second Sunday in July every year. Roy is the only living uncle. The rest have gone on to be with the Lord. We have lost two cousins, Martha Lewis Rideout and Daniel Kneeper.

This is a picture of the Hugh Lewis family in the 1940's. We, the grandchildren, have begun to arrive.

There are many stories I could tell about the Lewis family. Here are eight of my favorites:

After supper, Grandma would put the dirty dishes in the sink and cover the sink and go and be with Granddaddy. Someone asked her, "What if she died before morning and left the dirty dishes in the sink." Her reply, "That is one time I would get out of washing the dishes."

Grandma and Granddaddy would host teenage parties. A couple would decide to go outside. Granddaddy would go outside and talk to them until they decided to come back inside or leave.

Aunt Virginia said she would go to bed and worry that God's curtain would wear out. She said that Mama told her that God had a big curtain that He would draw at night to make it dark and that the moon and stars were holes in the curtain. Aunt Virginia thought the curtain was going to wear out. She knew the story was true because Aunt Virginia was not of school age, and Mama was going to school. I was born on Aunt Virginia's birthday. We celebrated many birthdays together.

My father was able to plant the straightest crop rows. Gordon would have crooked rows. He said that more grew in a crooked row than a straight row. Gordon was the oldest son. He took the leadership role of the family when my Granddaddy died. He took care of his younger brothers. The three brothers farmed together throughout their lives.

Mr. Sturdivant would come down and look for arrowheads in the field along the banks of the Nottoway River. Helen would walk with him and talk with him. Mr. Sturdivant introduced her to his son Bob (Robert). Bob and Helen were later married. Mama, Daddy, and Bob had passed away by the time I had Hepatitis C. I would go for treatments at the hospital and afterward go by Aunt Helens. When you left, she would stand at a door, windows, or outside and wave until you were out of sight.

Kitty (Katherine) had a coin playing with it, put it in her mouth, and accidentally swallowed it. She looked at the person who owned the coin and said, "Don't worry, I will give it back in two or three days." When Grandma died, Kitty gave up her job in Richmond and came back home to help Granddaddy and the family. After Granddaddy died, Kitty went back to work in Richmond. She would come out for the weekend and bring us Thalhimer's seven-layer cakes. She was the last of the seven to get married.

During the flood of the Nottoway River in 1940, Garnet was bitten by a black widow spider while at the woodpile. He came into the house and said, "I am good as dead." They went through the water to Huske and went to Stony Creek on a handcar on the railroad to the doctor. Garnett and Maggie Lou have a son a year younger than me and a daughter near my age. When I was young, I would get homesick. Their house was the only place I would stay. I would go up and help with tobacco during the summer.

Roy is eighteen years younger than my mother. He is the youngest child of Hugh and Pattie Lewis. There are many stories about him growing up. Roy used to ride his horse bareback, standing up. Roy was nine when Grandma died. He was fourteen when Granddaddy died. Granddaddy would read the Bible to Roy when he came to a word Granddaddy could not pronounce, Roy would tell him how to pronounce the word. Roy is retired.

Chapter 8

Lewis Mayes Meets Elaine Lewis

Granddaddy Lewis's cousin, Laura Hamilton, was living in the Taylor house. The Mayes' family was living in the Freeman house (Bonnie Doon). Daddy had a Model T. Mrs. Hamilton asked Daddy to carry her to see Hugh Lewis and family. Lewis sat on the porch and talked to Elaine while the older folks visited. He said Mama was the most talkative girl he had ever met, but he must have liked listening because he kept going back to see her. Mama and Daddy were married on August 1, 1936. The parsonage was vacant, so they moved in. The house was in disrepair with no electricity, running water, and indoor plumbing. Mama said that when they first moved in, they had to keep moving the bed to keep the plaster from falling onto the bed. They built a life together. Daddy farmed and worked various jobs while farming and, as we say, made a living. He bought a farm that included the parsonage and the old general store building that he used as a barn. Mama and Daddy worked hard and were able to remodel their home over the years.

My sister Dorothy Inez Mayes was born on March 10, 1938. She was born at home. She did not receive oxygen fast enough at birth, leaving her with mental health problems. When she went to school, the first-grade teacher locked her in a small bathroom as punishment. It caused her to have trauma. She fears being locked in still today. When we take her to Virginia Commonwealth University Medical College of Virginia Hospital (VCU-MCV) for an appointment in the morning, she would say, I hope they will not lock us in here. She never received a formal education, but she is very smart. She lived with Mama and Daddy until Daddy passed away on September 30, 1995. She lived with Mama until Mama died on December 25, 2003. Carol and I have lived across the road from the parsonage since 1993. Mama had strokes and was able to stay at home until she died because of Dot's help, and Carol and I helped from across the road. I am Dot's power of attorney. She came to live with us after Mama died. She fell and broke her ankle. They put in a plate with nine screws. She had to have rehab. Dot will not stay alone. We were paying sitters to keep her in the day while we worked. She went to rehab and found she liked the nursing home environment. A brief time after rehab, she went to live in an assisted living facility. Dot does not want to come back to live in Comans Well. She has had breast cancer. She fell and tore the ligaments in her leg away from her knee. She has other health problems. God has been faithful.

Pattie Mae Mayes was born on July 19, 1939. Pat was always on my side. You could not ask for a better big sister. She graduated in 1957 from Stoney Creek High School as one of seven graduates. She went to work at Yale Supply for Mr. Millard Magee. I remember one Christmas that I made out like a bandit. She would buy me a present, and I would see it, so she would give it to me and go buy me something else. This happened several times that year. Pat met Ted

Tracy Upton, and they were married on September 27, 1959. They had three children: Sylvia Mae, Ted Tracy Jr., and Walter Patrick. Pat graduated from John Tyler Community College. She kept books for Ted for many years. Ted and Pat divorced, she worked various jobs and since retired. She had a car accident a few years back, which broke her ankle. She has had multiple surgeries on her back and neck.

Walter, Ted Jr., and Pat were the first three people I baptized after I was ordained as a minister. Pat had been baptized in Sharon United Methodist Church. She and the boys came to Claremont Baptist Church, the first church I served as pastor. I baptized them in the James River.

Wamer Lewis Mayes was born on April 15, 1941. You could not ask for a better big brother, but he could tease you to death. When we were young, he had two personalities. He had one personality when Daddy was home and another personality when Daddy was away. When Daddy was home, he was an angel. When Daddy was away, he would keep the sisters and me yelling, "Mama, make him stop." All he had to do was look at us. Wamer grew up fast. He quit school and went to work at a service station. He farmed for a few years. He met Kathleen Morris, and they were married on January 4, 1963. The day they got married, the chimney of the parsonage caught fire. The chimney got so hot that the mantel on the closed-in fireplace caught fire. If the fire had started after they had left for the wedding, the parsonage would have burned down. Wamer left for the wedding with firemen on the roof. My Aunt Virginia said during the wedding she could smell smoke and wondered what was burning. Mama and Daddy's clothes had picked up the scent of smoke as they were getting ready. They had just fixed the upstairs as an apartment in the parsonage for Wamer and Kathleen. They have three sons: Wamer Lewis Jr., William Frederick, and Andrew Wade. Wamer began to paint houses for a living. I favored Wamer, and I have had people ask me to paint their house. Too bad no one offered to pay me for

Wamer's painting of his house. Wamer and Kathleen went to Hawaii on vacation before he died. He talked about the trip for the rest of his life. He really enjoyed the trip. In November 2010, Warmer died from an aneurysm that ruptured. God has been faithful.

Lewis and Elaine have a fourth child, me. I was born Hugh Patrick Mayes on September 11, 1948. I am the squeakiest wheel of all.

The fifth generation of the Mayes family lives in the parsonage now. Daniel and Tracy Pero live in the parsonage. Tracy is the great-granddaughter of Lewis and Elaine Mayes. The sixth generation of the Mayes family that I have known has been born. They are the great-great-grandchildren of Lewis and Elaine Mayes.

Daddy's smile and Model T won Mama's heart.

Chapter 9

1948 What a Tear?

The year began with Grandma and Granddaddy Mayes having to move. Granddaddy had discontinued farming the farm that the house was rented with. Mama and Daddy let them move in the parsonage with them. Mama had been told after Wamer was born not to have any more children. It had been almost seven years since Wamer was born, and then an accident, she was pregnant. Mama's health was always a squeaking wheel. The pregnancy was not an easy one. The new neighbors in the Freeman house (Bonnie Doon) were Raymond and Ida Ezelle. Ida was a nurse and gave Mama shots during her pregnancy.

Grandma Lewis had died in 1943 from a stroke. Granddaddy Lewis died on May 20, 1948, from a heart attack. Uncle Wilson Mayes died on June 16, 1948. Wilson was so weak when they took him to the hospital he could not walk by himself. Ida helped get Wilson from upstairs to the car. It was a stressful time for my pregnant Mama.

Mama told seven years old, Wamer, that he was going to have a baby sister or brother. He said, "I have two sisters, and I don't want another one. I am going to have a baby brother." She replied, "But it could be a little girl." He replied, "Mama, you and Daddy have nothing to do with this; I prayed for a little brother."

I was born Saturday, September 11, 1948, at 1:23 p.m. in Petersburg Hospital. Mama was unable to care for me at first. Annie Sesler, Daddy's first cousin, helped take care of me. Mama said I laughed and responded to Annie and looked at Mama like a stranger. I had pneumonia on the first of December 1948. Mama said that after she stayed with me in the hospital, I begin to respond to her. I have a bill from Petersburg Hospital, Inc. made out to Master Hugh P. Mayes for $46.75. I was in the hospital from December 1 to December 5 and was charged $9.25 a day for a total of $37.00. I was charged $1.75 for dressing and $8.00 for Penicillin for a total bill of $46.75.

Pauline Sesler Kennedy, Annie's daughter, had a project in school in Home Economics, and I was her project for her class. I am sure she got an A; it was such a good project. God has been faithful.

This is a picture of Granddaddy Mayes and Hillary Johnson sitting on the old parsonage front porch around the time I was born. There was no electricity or indoor plumbing. Thank God Daddy remodeled the house as I was growing up.

Chapter 10
Memories Before Six Years Old

In classes in college and seminary, I learned that the most important years of your life are the first five. I took a class in Theology and Self Understanding while I was in seminary. A fellow student looked at me and asked, "What are you taking the class for? You do not know anything about theology, and you will never understand yourself." We had to take a childhood memory and Bible passage and relate it to our story. I found out how important it is to how we guide children in their growing years. So many people see these as just babysitting years, but we are setting the foundation of a lifetime.

Many of my memories from early childhood have an element of fear. I can remember the room that Daddy would fix up as the kitchen had holes in the wall and seeing mice running in and out of the holes. I am afraid of mice. If I see a mouse, I buy mousetraps and poison to get rid of one. Wamer and Daddy would laugh at me for reacting to the sight of a mouse. Mama would reassure my fear. She would tell me how my Granddaddy Lewis was afraid of mice. She said that Daddy and Granddaddy were shucking corn by hand, and they uncovered a nest of mice. Daddy was using an ear of corn to kill the mice and was saying, "I got this one, Mr. Lewis, you get that one." Daddy turned so he could see Granddaddy, and Granddaddy was hopping from foot to the other foot. Mama loved her Daddy so much she made you want to be like him. I never faced my fear. I majored in college in sociology. I might have majored in psychology, but I was told you had to work with rats. I was in a drug and behavior psychology class, and the professor brought in three caged rats to show us how drugs would affect them. I sat in the front row of the class. I immediately got up and moved to the back of the class.

I remember that my Great Uncle John Velvin ran a store in Jarratt, Virginia. He had an accident and lost his leg and had a wooden leg.

I used to love to go to his store because he gave us candy. One night, thieves broke into his home, tied him and his sister up, and stole his safe. My Great Uncle John's wife had passed away, and my Great Aunt Bessie Belvin had come to live with him and keep house for him. They were Grandma Mayes's brother and sister. The day after the robbery, Mama, Daddy, and I went to Great Uncle John's house to visit. The whole time we were there, I was afraid the robbers were going to come back. Great Uncle John's gold pocket watch was stolen. The watch was recovered after he died. Daddy used the pocket watch for years. I have the pocket watch now.

After Great Uncle John died, Great Aunt Bessie moved back to Petersburg, Virginia. She had lived in Petersburg before she moved to Jarratt. I do not remember where, but I remember she had a darkroom you walked through and a black cat that did not like children. When we went to Jarratt to help her move back to Petersburg, she had that cat in a box. The cat was scratching the box and sticking its paw through the holes in the box. I was so scared that the cat was going to get out of the box. As I look back now, if I had only opened the box and let it run away, the problem would have been solved.

I remember a lady coming to the house to take the school census. I remember asking what she wanted to know. Mama explained that she wanted to know who was going to school and that I would be starting the next year. My reply was, I am not going to school.

I was wrong about that. I went to school for twenty-one years. I had no pre-school or kindergarten. I graduated from High School, Business College, Bachelor of Arts in Sociology, and a Master's of Divinity.

One night, Mama and Daddy went out with Uncle Garnett and Aunt Maggie Lou and left us at home with Uncle Roy. We children were playing, and somehow I fell back and hit my head on an iron bed. It made a cut in the back right side of my head. I still have the scare today, and if the barber does not cut my hair right, my hair will not lay right.

I remember the excitement of Uncle Roy and Aunt Violet getting married. I remember the wedding. The first wedding I ever went to.

Sharon United Methodist Church was having night services. My parents and I were sitting three or four rows from the back. Being Methodist, when the Lord's Supper is served, the congregation goes forward to the chancel rail. When my parents left me alone, I can remember being afraid. I was afraid someone might try and make me come up to the front since everyone seemed to be up there. I hid under the bench in fear and loneliness.

Annie Sesler had taken care of me after my birth. She lived next door to us in the Taylor house. Her daughter Pauline married John Kennedy of Stony Creek, Virginia. I remember Mama taking Annie to see Pauline after Pauline and John were married. Coming home, Mama ran off the culvert in front of Sappony Church and put Annie in the foot of the floor of the pickup. Annie was a fair size lady, and everyone laughed at the idea of Annie on the floor of the pickup. We did not have Sunday School at Sharon when I was very young, and we went to Fort Grove United Methodist Church for Sunday School. I remember the Sunday Mama came out of church crying because she heard that Annie had passed away.

An exciting day for me was when I was given a hand-me-down tricycle. I enjoyed riding in the yard. One day the pickup truck was parked in the yard, and I played that I was putting my tricycle under the garage like Daddy parked his vehicles under the garage. It was right behind the back wheel of the passenger side. I went into the house. Daddy got into the pickup truck and backed over the tricycle. He drove it to a local welder to have it fixed. When the welder brought it back, it wobbled and did not really ride that good. Mama began to cry. Trying to cheer her up, I said, "Look, Mama, it is doing the Tennessee Wig Walk. My mother always balanced things in the light of God. Her most quoted book behind the Bible was Pollyanna. "God wants you to be happy because if He did not, He would not have said so many times in His Word to be joyful. Look for the bright side of all things. There is always a bright side. There is always something to be glad and thankful for." Pollyanna theology may not be the best theology, but I know it brought one family through many trials.

Chapter 11

The Most Important Decision in Life

The most important decision you make in life is how do you respond to Jesus. I can remember being in Sunday School at Sharon United Methodist Church after starting school and being proud that I could print the name of Jesus. The only problem I made the "J" backward. Jesus loves us and wants a relationship with us and wants us to call upon His Name, even if we spell it with a backward J. Sharon United Methodist Church had summer revivals with Readville Baptist Church. The summers we had the revival at Sharon United Methodist Church, we had a Baptist preacher. The summers we had the revival at Readville Baptist Church, we had a Methodist preacher. I accepted Jesus as my Savior at the age of eight during a revival at Readville Baptist Church. I was baptized by Reverend R. L. Consolvo at Sharon United Methodist Church in 1956. It has been a long walk with Jesus. God has been faithful.

I remember two sermon illustrations from my growing-up years. During a hot summer revival in August before air condition in Sharon United Methodist Church, I remember a sermon by Reverend Ray Cutchins on hell. I was under ten years old. It was so hot in Church, and the setting was right for the sermon. The funeral home fans were well in use. For those of you who are of the air-conditioned generation, I will explain what a funeral home fan is. It is a seven by eight-piece of cardboard mounted on a wooden stick you used to fan yourself while the preacher preached. The front had a peaceful scene on it, and the back had the advertisement of a funeral home. Reverend Cutchins had a sermon illustration in which he said he had an elevator button, which he pushed to take you down to hell, where he interviewed several people. He interviewed a pilate, who continuously washed his hand, saying, "I cannot get this blood off my hands." He interviewed Judas, who continuously threw the thirty pieces of silver away. The sermon had a big impact on my faith. After I begin to preach, I had Reverend Cutchins come to Claremont and Shiloh to preach the message.

Hillary Johnson, who married my Daddy's first cousin, was a certified lay speaker for the United Methodist Church preached at Sharon when I was young. He used the illustration of a young girl picking a rose and carrying it to a lady whose house was a mess and giving it to her. The women took the rose a put in a vase. As the woman sat admiring the rose, she began to clean the table around the rose. This led to cleaning the room and the house. When we accept the Rose of Sharon, our Lord and Savior Jesus Christ, it leads us from a life of sin into the path of righteousness.

Praising the Lord at an early age.

Chapter 12

The Stony Creek School Years

I did not walk five miles in the snow to a one-room school, but I went from the first to the twelfth grade in the same building with the same principal. Our senior yearbook is titled *Creek Ripplings of 1966.* Our theme is "Our Treasured Memories". As I look back on these years, there are many treasured memories.

I was a timid, neurotic, young first grader. I had not quite had my sixth birthday. In my studies in college and seminary, I learned that the best way to become a neurotic is to have a neurotic mother in your first five years. My mother had a nervous breakdown after I was born. She tried all the avenues she could to get Dorothy's help. At ten, Dorothy was tested, and she was functioning at a five-year-old level. At one point, Mama was told to lock Dorothy away and forget she ever had her. Mama was close to her parents and family. Granddaddy Lewis died the year I was born. Uncle Wilson died the year I was born. Granddaddy and Grandma Mayes, Wilson, and Frances were living with Mama and Daddy the year I was born. My first caregiver, Annie Sesler, died in my early years. Mama told me that one day she went to the Nottaway River Bridge behind Granddaddy Lewis's house and threw all the narcotics that she had been prescribed into the river and said, "With God's help, I am going to make it." She did make it. Mama conquered her anxiety, but she continued to have physical problems. She had phlebitis and would have to stay in bed for weeks at a time. She fell off the tractor and broke a vertebra in her back and had to stay in bed for weeks. Since Grandma Lewis had died at age fifty-one, she thought she was going to die near fifty. These events had an effect on my developing psyche. In her later years, she still anguished over Dorothy's birth and only if she had been in a hospital. By then, I had met someone who had a son who was like Dorothy, who had been born in a hospital. I asked her to forgive herself; it was not her fault. She never mentioned it again. She lived to be almost eighty-eight.

We had many pets growing up. We had dogs, cats, and a duck. Puppies were born in the bus shed at school. Wamer came home with a puppy whose eyes were not opened. Daddy named the puppy Pug. Pug lived to be an old dog. Pug was a territorial dog. If the neighbor's dog came into our yard, Pug would chase him back to the line. Pug went to church more than a lot of people. The church being close by when a car would turn off of the road at the church; Pug would go to church. In the summer, before air condition, the doors to the sanctuary were left open. Pug would come in and lay under the back pew.

Dorothy brought home a duck. Someone gave the preacher's daughter two baby ducks. The ducks were not surviving well in the town of Stony Creek, so one ends up in Comans Well. Pug and Mr. Quack got along well most of the time. Mr. Quack would aggravate Pug and would grab Mr. Quack around the neck but would never hurt him.

Ida Ezelle Kitchen gave me a part Chihuahua puppy. Daddy always came up for our pet's name. He named him Poochie. Poochie became more Daddy's dog than mine. Daddy always went to bed early. Poochie stayed in the closed in back porch at night. Daddy would call and call. Poochie would not come. Daddy would go and get the shotgun and shoot up in the air. Poochie would almost knock Daddy down, getting on the porch. Aunt Edith Lewis, who lived across the road, would hear the shotgun blast and laugh and say, "Lewis is calling Poochie."

Looking at my report cards, I can trace my anxiety level through grades and attendance. My best years were third grade and my senior year. For the first three years, I had a security blanket at school. My big sister and brother and neighbor Betsy Bobbitt were there in school with me. I remember one time putting too much hair tonic on my hair. Pat and Betsy used all the tissues they had trying to get the tonic out of my hair as we rode the bus to school. Mrs. Florence Thornton wrote on my report card, "It has been a pleasure to teach Hugh. He's a most cooperative little boy." Mrs. Thornton was the wife of Earl Thornton, who ran the store as Sussex, Virginia, and was Post Master of Sussex.

I began having migraines while I was in the fourth grade. I missed eleven days. At the beginning of my fifth-grade year, I did not want to go back to school. I was sick. I missed seven days. Mama took me to the doctor. With the doctor's help, I finally decided that I could and would go to school. I learned to use my sense of humor and trusting God to get through my troubling times. I did not realize until now while writing this that I was truly suffering from separation anxiety. My migraine headaches started the year after my sister graduated from high school. My brother quit school and went to work in my fifth-grade year. I was away from the family. I was on my own. I had to realize that God was with me. When I was out of my safe zone of family, God was with me. When I was out of the village of Comans Well, God was with me. I only missed one day for the rest of the year. Remember, I lived in the old parsonage insight of Sharon Church. Comans Well had it all—God and family.

I remember I was in fifth or sixth grade when we had to draw a picture and put a person in it. I was not an artist. I never put a person in my drawings because I could not draw a good picture of a person. I drew the best person I could. Mrs. Lula Williams was my teacher. She taught me in fifth and sixth grade. She posted our pictures that we drew on the bulletin board. Mrs. Pearl Freeman was a teaching supervisor for the County of Sussex. She came to visit our class. She looked at our pictures on the bulletin board and looked at my picture and said, "That is the cutest monkey I ever saw." The whole class laughed because they knew it was supposed to be a person.

When the world laughs at you, laugh with it. I had drawn the best person I could. Mrs. Williams had a little flower garden out near the fence at school beside Route 40. She would take us out to work in it. I had a problem because if the flowers were not blooming, I did not know a flower from a weed. I was raised on the farm, and if it was not a peanut, it was a weed. Mini sermon—if you do not know Christ as your Savior, you are not a sheep, you are a goat. If you are not a peanut, you are a weed (Matthew 25:31–46). God knows if we are His children or not. We are all His creation, but we all are not His joint-heirs with Christ. Mrs. Freeman and Mrs. Williams both had family connections to Comans Well.

The grading scale changed the year I went into the seventh grade. It meant I dropped in my letter grades. I developed a negative attitude. If I thought I was not going to need it and it was boring, I did not apply myself and learn it. I did enough to get by. Daddy had to be at work early, and we got up early. I tried doing my homework in the morning but would run out of time. We only had heat in one room. It was hard to find quiet to do homework. With the old grading system, I would have never failed a class. I failed English in the eighth and tenth grades. In the tenth grade, I passed French I and I failed English. In the middle of my junior year, I felt the call to go to Business College. I had a reason to do better. My grades improved in the second semester. In my senior year, my grades were the best, and my attendance was one hundred and eighty days out of one hundred and eighty days.

I was on the first little league baseball team in the area. The Sussex Optimist sponsored our team. A representative came to school, and he asked the boys if they were interested in playing. I was excited and wanted to play. My Uncle Garnett gave me his old glove to play. I remember that first year, I got to stand in right field for an inning or two. I could catch the ball, but heaven only knew where it was going when I threw it. I began playing first base.

I earned money in the summer, working on the farm. One year, I took the money and bought myself a first baseman's mitt. The boys on the team made fun of my glove and called it a piece of plywood, but I could snag a ball in it. I remember one time we were playing Claremont; everyone was yelling about the umpire and saying he could not see. I got up to bat and struck out. I turned and told the umpire he was blind and could not see. Mr. Sam Lilley took me aside and talked to me. What a life lesson. I later in life became pastor of Claremont Baptist Church. I met a man that remembered the little league days. I asked him did he ever umpire. He said no. I was going to apologize. Today, it is becoming a major problem, according to the news of parents becoming a problem at a sporting event. I played little and pony league as long as I was eligible. I played baseball for three years in high school. I never yelled at an umpire again. I could drive and would go home to work. I did not play my senior year.

I built a backboard and set up a basketball goal. I shot basketball. It was something I could do alone. There was no one around. I played basketball in my ninth and tenth year in high school. We did not have a gym. We practiced on an asphalt court. Our home games were played at Waverly High School. My freshman year, our coach, Mr. Wright, gave me an award for being the most improved player. He said, "When he first saw Hugh, I did not think he could chew gum and walk at the same time." Notice I do not chew gum. I had made the team, and in my sophomore year, I played enough to earn a high school letter. During my junior year, we had a new coach. The first practice, he gave us a rigorous exercise workout. I was out of shape. I became sick and went and laid on the bathroom floor. I decided if I could not do the exercises, I should not make the team. It was peanut harvesting season. I drove to school; then I would leave early and went home to work.

In the early 1960s, the first new residence in my lifetime was added to Comans Well. My Great Uncle Clifford and Aunt Edith purchased a lot from Daddy and Mama and purchased a mobile home. Uncle Clifford was my Grandfather Hugh Lewis's brother and a World War I Veteran. He was retired from Hunter Holmes McGuire VA Medical Center, Richmond, Virginia. He worked in maintenance in the old hospital. I drove Uncle Clifford's car to get my driver's license. His car was smaller than Daddy's 1959 Chevrolet and did not have the wings of a 1959 Chevrolet. Uncle Clifford and Aunt Edith went to Billings, Montana, to visit his daughter in 1964. They wanted me to go to help with the driving. I stayed home to chop peanuts and put in tobacco to earn spending money. I stayed home and made money instead of spending money. The first year we had Daylight Saving Time part, or Virginia had it and part of the state stayed on Eastern Standard Time. Aunt Edith and Uncle

Clifford were still living in Colonial Heights. They would come out to see us, and by standard time, they would get here before they left home. Going home, they lost an hour. Daddy said he would never set his clock up. He never set the mantle clock up in his bedroom or his pocket watch. He kept his word for over thirty years until his death in 1995.

November 22, 1963 was one of the most memorable days in high school. It was the day that President John Kennedy was shot. We were in French class when Mr. Gilbert came on the loudspeaker and made the announcement. Mr. Gilbert had sent home one of our classmates that day for disciplinary problems. When the classmate heard the news on television, he called back to school. Mr. Gilbert went home and listened to the television before he would make the announcement.

> It is very seldom that a teacher is recognized by his students for his teaching ability. We, the annual staff, feel, however, that Mr. Wright is completely deserving of our thanks. In his classes, one finds the kind of instruction that makes one completely familiar with the subject. Out of class, he presents a picture of one to be admired. Whether coaching basketball and forensics or drawing animal-like maps and diagrams, Mr. Wright has given our school something which will always be remembered. We can only wish him luck and God-speed wherever he goes. With great admiration and appreciation, we present you, Mr. Wright, with your copy of the *1964 Creek Ripplings*.[68]

Mr. B. J. Wright was an inspiration to me. He came to Stony Creek second semester of our eighth-grade year and stayed through our sophomore year. He coached boys' baseball and basketball. He was active in all school and community activities. He taught social

---

[68] Creek Ripplings: Moments To Remember. 1964. Volume XVI. Stony Creek, Virginia: Stony Creek High School.

studies and physical education. He taught me to throw a baseball better. Mike Gorbenko started calling me Baby Huey after Donald Duck's nephew while we were in elementary school. Over the years, it became Hughtie Baby. Mr. Wright picked up on my nickname, and that became my name. Other teachers, students, parents called me Hughtie Baby. Years after graduation, it has been to some my name. Even though I was not the best in sports or grades, he encouraged me and gave me confidence. He helped me out of my introvert ways to become more extroverted. He started the serving of hamburgers and refreshments in the school cafeteria after basketball games. Even though he left Stony Creek before my junior year, I used him as a reference to Smithdeal-Massey Business College.

Mr. E. V. Gilbert was our principal for all twelve years of school. You did not want to go to the principal's office because that is where you were sent if you misbehaved. I never got sent to the office for behavior. During our junior year, Stony Creek and Jarratt High Schools were merged into one at Stony Creek. We had grades first, second, and eighth thru twelve. Mr. Wright had left the year before. I suggested that our class take on the project of serving after the basketball games. I would get soft drinks and ice them after school, and different parents would make sweets to sell and chaperone. We would cook hamburgers to sell. Mr. Gilbert would give me the key to school when I left on Friday, and I would return it on Monday morning. The first time we served, we were ready to cook the hamburgers, but nobody knew what to cook the hamburgers in. The top of the stove was flat like a grill, so we cooked them on the flat top. We wiped the grease off the best we could. Monday morning, Mr. Gilbert came and got me out of class and took me to the cafeteria where the cafeteria ladies showed me the pans that we were supposed to use. They said we could have burned the school down.

I was in the senior play. I was vice-president of the senior class. We graduated on June 6, 1966 (6/6/66).

This is a picture of my brother Wamer with a side view of Bonnie Doon in the background. My Mayes grandparents were living there at the time. Wamer is ready for a snowball fight.

Chapter 13

The Smithdeal-Massey Years

In the sixties, there were some very dry years. Daddy worked in the logwoods and farmed. The farm lost money. There was a change in the Bank of Southside officers in 1965. Daddy seemed to lose confidence in his borrowing power. He would tell me, "I am not going to mortgage the farm for you to go to school."

I started chopping peanuts at an early age. Daddy had started plowing with a mule when he was big enough to hold the plow. Daddy would put me on someone's row. I would chop until they caught up with me and had checked to see if I had pulled all the grass. When I became good enough, I had my own row. Daddy paid me like the hired help, $5 a day. I graduated from driving the tractor and other farm work. In the summer, when the tobacco would be harvested, I would go up and help my uncles. I saved my money. Daddy gave me $2 a week for school lunch. Lunch was thirty cents, and I was left with fifty cents. In my high school years, I did not eat lunch. I kept the $2 for spending money. I used the money saved from working in the summer and the lunch money for spending money throughout the year.

I prayed about my career, and the door opened for me to attend Business College. I felt called to go to Smithdeal-Massey. The farm was not big enough to support me. I had felt called to the ministry, but I did not have the grades or the money to go to college. My cousin, Patsy Sturdivant, was going to Smithdeal-Massey, and I was allergic to smoke, dust, etc. on the farm; I decided that it was for me. I made the decision mid-way through my junior year. I changed from the academic program in high school to the general program. In my senior year, I got an "A+" for the year in Bookkeeping.

In March of 1966, I had to send in $15. I did not have it. I received a graduation gift of $15. I went to a man in the community,

Mr. Millard Magee, and asked if he would help me get a loan from one of the banks with which he was associated. He did. The Bank of Waverly financed my going to Smithdeal-Massey. They asked me if Daddy would co-sign because it would look better. It was an open note, and Daddy co-signed. I worked at the boarding house cleaning bathrooms and light cleaning to earn my room and board.

I graduated from high school on Monday, June 6, 1966. I started Smithdeal-Massey Business College the following Monday. My big beach trip was to Moore's Lake for part of a day. I earned an Accounting with Automation Diploma. It was an eighteen-month program. By going to night school, I completed the program in fifteen straight months. I was out of Business College in September 1967.

What a rude awakening this country boy, who had never crossed a city street without a walk sign (Petersburg, Virginia), had in the fan district of Richmond. People were engaging in sins that I did not know existed. I was out of my comfort zone of Comans Well. Our lives were based on God, family, and community. In Richmond, everyone seemed to fend for oneself. People solicited me regularly for money or sex. One day I was walking a few blocks from the college, and two men in a car started following me slowly and yelled to me. I kept walking. They got ahead of me and pulled to the curb, and the man on the passenger side stated that they wanted to talk to me. I kept walking and crossed the street and headed down a one-way street so they could not follow me. They went to the next block and came around to meet me. I took off running and ran until I entered the building where I was living. It is better to be a chicken than a dead duck.

I began to have migraine headaches again. They came back with a vengeance. They were worse and more often. I started seeing a doctor in Richmond. The first time I saw him, I was in the middle of a full, blown migraine, vomiting, diarrhea, and blurred vision. He said he was not sure what I had but to come back the next day that I would be a lot better or a lot worst and that I could not stay in the condition I was in for very long. The doctor began giving me tranquilizers. He sent me to a neurologist. He prescribed a stronger medication—Darvon.

Chapter 14

State Planter Bank Years

I finished Business College and turned nineteen in September 1967. I started work as a unit record operator trainee. I had seen State Planters Bank advertisements on television, and I was excited about my new job. My hours were noon to 8:30 p.m. My first job was making loan coupon books with IBM eighty column cards, printing loan letters, and mailing them. While I was with State Planters Bank, we became United Virginia Bank. I believe we were the first company to get a voice response computer in the area. I remember taking Mom and Dad to Richmond to an open house at the bank to hear the computer talk.

I roomed in a house on Park Avenue. I owed $2,600 for my business college education. I was anxious to get a car. I did not like riding the bus at night and walking four blocks to the room. I had to catch a bus home and a ride with someone or ride a bus back to Richmond. I was able to finance a 1968 Volkswagen sedan for a total cash price of $1,798.75 with The Bank of Waverly. I still have the sales invoice.

I had been working for five months when I had a premonition of death. I was sitting in my room in Richmond when a cold feeling came over me, and I saw my mother packing my belongings as though I were dead. The following Thursday, my lung collapsed. I was in pain when I came home from work. I could not lie down. I called the doctor I had been seeing, and he told me to go to a hospital that I did not know how to find. I went to the nearest hospital to me. They did not take emergencies and gave me directions to Saint Mary's Hospital. They called in a thoracic specialist. He inserted a chest tube. I was under twenty-one, so they had to call my parents for consent. My parents came on Friday.

It was a busy hospital day. I remember on Friday night getting very weak and throwing up. I did not call for a nurse. I remember thinking I saw a sign above my bed, Angelic Door. I felt that I was going to pass through the door to heaven. I was not found until the next morning in a state of blood pressure shock. I was moved into intensive care.

I had never heard of intensive care. I could see and hear people, but I could not communicate back. I wondered why visitors would come in and almost immediately go out. I was given eight pints of blood and stayed in intensive care for three days. I had three IVs, two for blood and one for glucose. I remember the effort it took to sit up the first time and the excitement of the nurses that I was able to sit up. The doctors were discussing removing my lung when, miraculously, it stopped bleeding and began to function. After I was back in a regular room, the doctor inserted a needle in my back to drain fluid. I was in the hospital for two weeks. I had to work for three months before I would have health insurance. Praise the Lord; I had just received health insurance. God has been faithful.

Soon after I returned to work, I was examined for the Army. It was the Vietnam era, and many my age were getting drafted. I was six feet, one inch tall and weighed 118 pounds. I was underweight, plus I had had a lung collapse. They re-examined me in six months, and I was given a 4F—not able to serve.

Chapter 15

The Volkswagen Years

When I returned home from the hospital, people told me how thankful I should be that God had left me for a purpose. I agreed, but I did not know what the purpose was. I began to build a circle of friends and reconnect with a social life. After I had graduated from high school, I had focused on Business College. I came home to Comans Well every weekend, but only went wherever my parents went. My social life was put on hold. I still attended church and began to teach Sunday School.

In the summer of 1968, a group of us would meet at M. W. Dunn's store and softball field to play softball. I was driving friends' home after playing softball when smoke began coming out of the dash of the Volkswagen and it shut off. We rolled to the side of the road and stopped. I told Bert Parker to stay with the car, and Charles Parker and I would walk to the service station that was in sight. I called my cousin, H. G. Lewis, to come pick us up. I looked up, and I saw Bert driving into the parking lot of the service station. He said that he was standing behind the car when the lights started flashing and the car started up. He got in and drove it up to the service station. I tried to turn the car off, and it would not turn off. I tried to choke it off, and it would not go off. We finally had to take the cables off the battery to get the car to turn off. My uncles loaded the car on their farm truck and hauled it to Richmond for me. Ward Volkswagen had to replace the electrical system in my car. I believe my Volkswagen had a mind of its own like Herbie the Love Bug.

People gave me rides to Richmond when I was at Smithdeal-Massey, so when I received the Volkswagen back, I drove people to and from Richmond. Some Sunday nights, I had four passengers and their luggage in my "bug". Sometime on Saturday night, my cousins, Martha Lewis, Cindy Lewis, Roy Lewis Jr., and friends Judy

Warf, Billy Houchins, would ride around singing. Cindy played the guitar, and the rest sang. Roy Jr. would sit straddling the gearshift and would shift the gears as I pushed in the clutch. I loved music. In my teen years, I had a pocket transistor radio that I carried with me when working or walking on the farm. I carried the transistor radio to Business College. The Volkswagen did not have a radio when I bought it. I had a radio installed as soon as I could afford it.

Chapter 16

Music

Having an older brother and sisters, I was exposed to their music. I was using Revelation 3:20 (NIV), "Here I am! I stand at the door and knock. If anyone hears my voice and opens the door, I will come in and eat with that person, and they with me." As I was thinking about this verse, the line I hear you knocking but you can't come in. I could not remember the song, but I remembered the line from over fifty years ago. I concluded that this is the problem with people today. As Jesus knocks on their heart door, they will not let Him in. The problem is not Jesus but the people who will not listen to the call of God. I googled the line, "I hear you knocking, but you can't come in," and it was a song by Fats Domino.[69] I remember as a teenager singing to an album I had of his. I would go to my room and perform the songs on the records. I had no audience. It did not injure anyone. They say I burn up the wires to the nursery. Music is the universal language. We better be careful about what we listen to. My parents and I went to Florida with Johnny and Belle Jarratt, Woody, and Catherine Dunn. Mama would hear "Blueberry Hill" by Fats Domino, and she would tear up; she missed the other children so much. We were only gone for four days.

My brother Wamer took me twice to the Mosque Theater to see the Dick Clark Caravan of stars. I was the younger tag along, but I loved it. While I was in Smithdeal-Massey, I would stay over on Friday nights to go to concerts. I saw the Righteous Brothers and The Dave Clark Five in separate concerts. As time passed, I took the Volkswagen singing group to concerts. Martha was married and moved to Florida, but the other five of us or some of us went to many concerts. To name

---

[69] "I Hear You Knocking Written by Dave Bartholomew and Pearl King, 1955." n.d. Lyrics.Com. 2020. https://www.lyrics.com/lyric/16409252/Dave+Edmunds/I+Hear+You+Knocking.

some of the concerts we went to—The 5th Dimension, Three Dog Night, Chicago, Sonny and Cher, Leon Russell, and Jethro Tull. We went to the Mosque Theater, the Richmond Coliseum, the Hampton Coliseum, and the Norfolk Scope to concerts. We also went to the Virginia Squire Basketball games.

Chapter 17

Tragedy

When you are young, you think death is for old people. You do not think of young people dying. My Mayes grandparents and their brother and sisters died. I went to the funerals growing up, but they were old. It was their time. But when six young people were killed in five car accidents that had an impact on my life.

I was in early high school when George Crowder was killed in an accident. He was the son of Mac Crowder. Mr. Crowder owned the farm across the Nottoway River from my Lewis uncles. His son would come up from Florida to stay during the summer. I would see George from time to time. He was killed on the Fourth of July in an accident. He was about my size, and I was given his clothes. I was not too thrilled about wearing the clothes, but I needed clothes, so I wore them.

Thomas Fannin, Jr. was a year ahead of me in high school. He decided he wanted to attend Smithdeal-Massey. He was going to stay at the same boarding house that I was staying in. He was killed in an accident just before the quarter he was supposed to start. I notified Smithdeal-Massey of his death.

In my junior and senior years, I had to ride the elementary bus headed to Jarratt to Yale, transfer to the high school bus headed to Stony Creek. Jean Hogwood was five grades behind me, and Charlotte Hogwood was eight grades behind me. Jean sat in a seat behind me and always liked to talk. Charlotte always spoke. Jean had become of driving age, and on the way to meet the school bus, they were killed in an accident. I felt so sorry for their parents losing their only two children in an accident.

Bert Parker became my best friend after I graduated from Smithdeal-Massey. He dated a girl that lived near me, and I dated a girl that lived near him. He worked at Stony Creek on weekends. He would come and stay with our family. He was killed on December 20, 1969, in an accident.

Audrey Ezelle was the little girl next door. She was a couple of years younger than I. She was the cause of most of my whippings, not that I got that many. I was not supposed to hit a girl. She would get mad, and her fist would fly. I let it go most of the time, but sometimes I would get tired of it and hit her back. If Daddy saw me, I was going to get a whipping.

One night I came in about 1:00 a.m. from work, and there were lights on in the Taylor house and cars in the yard. Daddy came out of the parsonage and told me Audrey had been killed in an accident. I went over to the Taylor house. Sallie Bobbitt and I spent the rest of the night with Ida and Raymond Ezelle. These young deaths definitely had an effect on me.

Chapter 18

A Step Closer to God

I had been teaching the teenage class at Sharon United Methodist Church for a while. I felt I was not reaching the teenagers and decided to change churches and go to Sappony Baptist. Sappony Baptist was my mother's family church. I was active with my cousins everyday life and participated in the church activities, so I decided to move my membership. I had always wanted to be baptized like Jesus, so I was happy to be immersed. I was baptized on July 11, 1971.

I began actively working with the young people. I purchased a slate bed pool table and put it in a building at my uncles. The preacher would come, and we would have Bible study, refreshments, and shoot pool. It was a safe place for the teenagers to go. We would go by Davis' Restaurant after shooting pool or after Church. There was a song the young people found out that I liked and would play on the jukebox. Kris Kristofferson had released *Why Me* in 1972. The song spoke to me. I, a sinner, had done nothing to deserve the blessing of God; He just gives them to us. Years later, I saw one of the waitresses from the restaurant; she reminded me how we always played *Why Me*.

My music choice had begun to change. Some of the last rock concerts I attended, you could smell marijuana. I gave up the concert scene. I always liked the hymns and Christian music. I loved George Beverly Shea singing *How Great Thou Art.* I loved Tennessee Ernie Ford singing *Peace in the Valley.* I loved Elvis Presley singing *Crying in the Chapel.* I loved to hear Pauline Kennedy sing a solo in church. I loved the fact that Roy Jr. played the piano for church and that Cindy played the guitar and sang for special music for church.

In October 1973, God called me to preach again, stronger than before. One Sunday night, our church was having a gospel sing. We had celebrated the church's bi-centennial earlier that year and had a gospel group for the afternoon service, but I left.

When I was young, living at home with my parents, we used to watch gospel music before we went to church. At this time in life, working shift work, I was just glad to get up and get to church on time. I went this particular night out of respect for John and Pauline Kennedy. I went to support them because they had invited the group. I wanted to support them because they had supported my work with the young people. I went with the idea that I could survive the little concert while this rinky-dink group would be singing. I had forgotten my early love of gospel music.

I was surprised to find a Silver Eagle bus parked in the church parking lot. I offered to help carry in the equipment. I said, "Give me something I cannot break. I will carry it in." When it was time to sing, to my surprise, the church was full. I had gone because I was afraid nobody would show up. The church was so full that I sat in the balcony. The pastor stood up and introduced The Hopper Brothers and Connie. Little did I know that this would be the night that changed my life completely.

I heard God talked about in a personal way that I had never heard before in their testimonies. I heard God sung about with so much expression and love that I had never heard before. As I looked down into their faces and saw love, joy, and peace that I lacked in my life, God spoke to me in a mighty way. I did not respond to the altar call, but I knew in my heart God wanted me in His ministry. Beware God can use methods and people for His purpose even if we do not think He can. God has been faithful.

It took until the following March, during a revival led by Reverend Rolland Powell, that I would respond to the call into ministry at the altar. I asked the young people what they wanted to do as a group. They said to have the Hopper Brothers and Connie come back to church. I called Claude, and the group came back in the spring of 1974.

The group sang a lot in the Richmond area. I started going to see them whenever they were close by. They were at the Mosque Theater in Richmond periodically. I remember having a 1974 Pinto Station Wagon; the passenger door would not close tight. I tied the door shut and drove to the concert. Claude asked me would I drive him to a nearby fast food to get something to eat. He comes out with Ed O'Neil of The Dixie Melody Boys to get in the car. I was embarrassed to put Ed in the back seat as tall as he is and tie the front door shut. I had had several good cars and had purchased the Pinto to save money, and all I had with it was problems.

Gospel music became the only music I listened to. I gave away my collection of rock music and recorded over some of the eight tracks with gospel music. *One Day at a Time* soon became my theme song, as sung by The Hopper Brothers and Connie.

Chapter 19

I Was a Train Wreck

In six years, I had gone from a unit record operator trainee to a computer operations supervisor for the largest stock brokerage firm in the Southeast based outside of New York, Wheat First Securities. I had tripled my salary. I had purchased a mobile home. I had purchased a color television (I only knew a few people who had one at the time) and stereo equipment.

I had a 1970 Nova, a 1971 Chevelle, 1972 Grand Torino Sport, 1973 factory ordered Grand Torino Sport, and in 1974 went back to a 1974 Pinto Station Wagon. When I ordered the 1973 Grand Torino Sport, I thought I was going to have the coolest car in the area. It was loaded for that day and time. It had an automatic in the floor. I wanted four in the floor, but I was under twenty-five, and I didn't want to pay the extra insurance.

When I had the Volkswagen at a stoplight, I would take off and shift the gears real fast to get to the speed limit and laugh at the car beside me, taking off like we were racing. I could not win a race with a sports car with my Volkswagen. Maybe it is good I did not get four in the floor.

Before I acquired my car, a young lady in the church family purchased a car with four in the floor. An older man who lived four miles from me purchased a Grand Torino, the same color with a laser strip like the car I had ordered. So much for having the coolest car in the area. The 1974 Pinto taught me to praise God for a car that runs.

The Hopper Brothers and Connie were in Richmond in the spring of 1974, while I had the 1973 Grand Torino Sport. They were singing for a revival. I picked Roger Talley up one morning, and he took me to work and kept the car for the day. I caught a city bus to the concert that night. At least someone had seen me in a car without the door tied together.

I was on the run. I picked my mother's thought of dying at fifty and turned it into I am going to die young. Uncle Wilson had died at thirty-one. Uncle Wilson died with his lungs filling with fluid. I had had the lung collapse, and I still hurt on the left side. I weighed 118 pounds. The average weight with my height is 144 to 188. My blood pressure was 90/60. The average blood pressure for my age was 120/79. I would have chest pains, and I would go to the hospital emergency room.

One night, I left work and went to the emergency room. The doctor caught on an x-ray a problem with my lung. She wanted me to stay in the emergency room overnight. I was living in Comans Well. Comans Well is fifty-three miles from downtown Richmond. I asked could I go to a motel close by. She said, "Yes."

A Gideon Bible and I had a prayer meeting. I returned to the hospital the next morning. I was released to go home. I was having migraines. When my eyes would blur, I knew it would not be long before I would start vomiting. I would check into a motel. I had Darvon pills that I would take as soon as I arrived in the motel. I would call home to my parent's house to tell them I would not be coming home so they would not worry. I was living across the road at the time. Mama would always call and get someone to come with her to get my car and me. I would be too sick to drive. I would have bronchitis. I went to the doctor regularly. I just did not have the stamina I should have. I was given B12 shots regularly.

One time the doctor gave me seven pills for one a day. They gave me energy. I was really active. I lost seven pounds that week. Those pills became history real fast. Flash-forward to the year 2000, when I was diagnosed with hepatitis C, the virus was living in me. I contracted the virus from the blood transfusions in 1968. Flash forward to the year 2015, when it was discovered that I had a hole in my heart. The blood coming back from the body passes through the heart, goes to the lungs to be oxygenated, and back through the heart to go back out to the body. The blood was going through the hole and back out to the body without getting oxygenated. I had lived the first sixty-six years of my life with an oxygen level that VCU-MCV Medical Center would not let me out of the trauma intensive care. Flash forward to 2015, I found I have a negative reaction to narcotics.

I was working shift work. I was not getting enough rest. For periods of time, I worked eighty hours a week, seven days a week. Overtime was not an option. It was my job; the work had to be done. We would have computer conversions or software changes that created longer hours. We had a nightly run that took fourteen hours. We started at five p.m. and ran until completed. I have worked twenty-four hours straight. One of the computers we had had three vendors. Keep in mind these were huge mainframe computers. I called the vendor that we were getting error messages on, and the civil engineer would come and say, "No, it is one of the other vendors' problem." We called that vendor.

One time, we had to have a civil engineer flown into Richmond. I kept a pillow on the console of the car and would go get it and sleep on the floor of one of the offices until the computer was fixed. I remember being so fragile emotionally that I tried having a pet. Just before I was to leave for work, a log truck hit and killed my dog. I went back into the house and called work and quit without any notice. I had lost my friends in death, my social life was near none, and I was working seven days a week with no church. I had enough. I quit.

The next day, a Saturday, my boss and a friend from work came to Comans Well and talked me into coming back to work. I was asked to move back to Richmond to be close to work. I had my mobile home in Comans Well and shared an apartment in Richmond. The young man worked opposite shifts. We seldom saw each other at the apartment. I became more alone. I felt like a sinking ship. I really did not care about a computer career anymore. All I wanted to do was to serve God. I could not walk out and leave my debts, so I began to try to save and come out of debt.

During the oil embargo, gas jumped in price; you could only buy gas on an odd day or an even day, whichever day you were assigned. The stock market dropped. We had to start cutting corners. We had finally gotten a fully trained staff to cover the twenty-four hours a day. I was finally not working so many hours.

In May 1974, I was told I had to lay someone off. We had a new manager over me. I had told him we did not need as many people as we were hiring. Yes, it was nice, but we were getting overstaffed. It came down from upper management; I had to lay someone off. I had friends at Media General, who I knew would hire me. My immediate boss and I did not get along that well, so I decided to take the layoff myself. I took a $1,600 a year salary cut. The first thing I did was sublease the apartment and move back to Comans Well.

Chapter 20

Do Not Try This at Home or Ever

The newfound sense of call that I had felt in October and had responded to in March was overshadowed in the problems of the summer of 1974. My only desire in life had been to make a moderate living, to have a family, and to serve God. I had made good money compared to the fifty-cent an hour chopping peanuts or my starting salary of $300 a month. I spent the money on things and gave part of it away. Staring death in the face with my lung collapsed and losing six friends in death, I was grabbing as much of life as fast as I could, as fast as my stamina would allow.

After the job lay off and the reality of how in debt I was, I went into a deep depression. I felt like a complete failure. I had lost my girlfriend. I had asked her to marry me, and she had said no. I know now that it was a good decision on her part. I had lost my job and a good income. All that overtime made money, but it added to my health problem. I felt I had failed God. The call I felt to preach did not seem to be going anywhere. I could not find a reason to live in drinking, in drugs (legal or illegal), illicit sex, or the party life.

On July 18, 1974, I decided to commit suicide. I left work and stopped by a Seven-Eleven and bought two beers. I had never tasted a beer, but I had heard if you mixed alcohol and pills, it would kill you. I stopped about three miles from home on a dirt road at Howell's Mill Pond. I drank one beer. It tasted so bad; I threw the other one into the pond. I went home and took all the prescription drugs I had.

I did not count the pills as I took them, but by the empty pill bottles, I took the following: a year-old bottle of tranquilizers, about twenty-five aspirin, eight Minocin capsules, eight to twelve Darvon pills. I said and still say, what better way to go in the rapture than listening to The Hopper Brothers and Connie (The Hoppers). I decided to play a tape. As soon as I started listening to the tape, I started praying. I did not pray for God to keep me alive, but I asked God to forgive me for taking my life, and for all my sins and failures. A peace came over me, and I wanted to go to church.

I drove fourteen miles to Sappony Baptist Church. The last thing I remember was lying down on the floor of my Sunday school room. The next thirty-six hours are a blank to me. Somehow, when I woke up enough to realize it was daylight and morning, I drove home. I do remember vomiting at one point, and that probably got rid of a lot of the pills. I began to wake up to consciousness on Saturday afternoon. I had taken the drugs on Thursday evening. When I began to really wake up, I told the family what I had done. They drove me to the emergency room at Saint Mary's hospital. By the time I arrived at the hospital, I was fully awake and ashamed of what I had done. I told the doctor I had taken only a few too many of the Darvon capsules. The doctor said I had taken the wrong medicine and gave me a new prescription. I never filled the prescription and went to my primary care doctor on Monday. I was admitted to the hospital in Emporia.

Chapter 21

It's Time to Preach

Mama's question was, "With your faith, why in the world would you do such a thing?" I have been searching for an answer for forty-four years. Through college and seminary, I have written papers on suicide. I studied the statistics. I majored in sociology and had eighteen hours of psychology. I took pastoral care classes in seminary. My best answer is that I was overwhelmed with my day-to-day life, and I lost hope in the future. I could see no way of achieving my goals of ministry.

I had put limits on what God can do in my life. My advice to anyone with suicidal thoughts is to let go and let *Jesus, Take the Wheel.* Will Hopper stated that a lifeguard could not save a person from drowning until the victim stopped fighting and let the lifeguard save him. God could not help me as long as I was trying to do His will my way. I stopped putting limits on the rest of my life according to the circumstances of today. I stopped putting limits on God. I read George Mueller's book *Answer to Prayer.* I started a new prayer life.

From sociology and psychology, I learned the importance of a circle of friends. Find someone to talk to who accepts you for who you are. God created us as social beings. Express your need for love and acceptance. Be genuine with your feelings. Keep reaching out until someone helps you. Keep God and church in the center of our life. Spend time with God each day. If I had died, I would have missed out on so many years of God's blessings here on earth.

One of the greatest helps in my life is listening to gospel music. Every song has a message. The songs turn your thoughts toward Jesus and God. God speaks to you through the Holy Spirit. Music is the universal language. Feed your soul with songs about God. A gospel song will lift you up and change you from pouting and being depressed to praising and thanking God for the blessings He has given you. Gospel singers have been great friends and inspirational. Read and study God's love letter to you, the Bible. Read on to the end of the book to see how God has been faithful in my life.

We all go through times when everything seems to be coming at us at once. We may feel like we're drowning. Whether we call it "the blues" or full-blown depression, we feel overwhelmed. Biblical leaders, historical figures, and great preachers all have experienced times of overwhelming despair and hopelessness.

- Moses. Moses felt so fed up with the Israelites' endless complaining he urged God, "And if thou deal thus with me, kill me, I pray thee, out of hand, if I have found favour in thy sight; and let me not see my wretchedness" (Numbers 11:15 KJV).
- Elijah. Elijah was so overwhelmed with his fear of Jezebel that he prayed, "...It is enough; now, O Lord, take away my life; for I am not better than my fathers" (1 Kings 19:4 KJV).
- Abraham Lincoln. As a lawyer in the Midwest, Abraham Lincoln suffered such depression that his friends kept all knives and razor blades away from him for a time for fear he might commit suicide. He wrote, "I am now the most miserable man living. If what I feel were equally distributed to the whole human family, there would not be one cheerful face on earth (...) To remain as I am is impossible. I must die or be better."[70]
- Charles Haddon Spurgeon. The great preacher from London was plagued with depression: "I, of all men, am perhaps the subject of the deepest depression at times (...) I am the subject of depression so fearful that I hope none of you ever get to such extremes of wretchedness as I go to."[71]

---

[70] "Quote by Abraham Lincoln." n.d. Quotetab. 2020. https://www.quotetab.com/quote/by-abraham-lincoln/i-am-now-the-most-miserable-man-living-if-what-i-feel-equally-distributed-to-the?source=men.

[71] Ethridge, Grant. 2018. "Bible Studies for Life: KJV Adults" 6 (2): 110.

God worked in their lives and brought them through. God worked in my life and brought me through. God will work in your life. Just trust Him, obey Him, and walk with Him.

Chapter 22

Picking Up the Pieces

Soon after I was released from the hospital, a group of us from church went to Watermelon Park near Berryville, Virginia. The Hopper Brothers and Connie had a weekend singing with multi-groups, preaching, and baptism in the Shenandoah River.

The rest in the hospital, if you can call it that with all the tests, the counseling of pastors and Dr. Thomas A. Walker, followed by a Spirit-filled weekend at Watermelon Park, gave me a new perspective on life. I returned home and to work with a stronger commitment to God.

My theme song was and is *One Day a Time*. Some days were really trying. Sunday, August 25, 1974, was one of those days. A group of us went to a drive-in movie the night before. My transmission on the Pinto station wagon began to slip. The car had to be pushed to get moving to go home.

On Sunday morning, I asked Daddy could I borrow his pickup to go to Sappony Church. After church, Henry Gill and Danny Young were going home with me to spend the afternoon. They asked could they ride in the back of the pickup. They were farm boys used to riding in the back of a pickup, and Henry would ride on the back of a spreader truck shoveling plaster on peanuts, so I said yes. I made a ninety-degree turn onto a dirt road, and I looked up into the rearview mirror, and Henry was running behind the pickup. He had fallen out the back of the pickup. He had a gash on his back that needed stitches. Someone asked me later if I called an ambulance. "No, I turned around and took him to the hospital." He was underage. It was his fifteenth birthday weekend. We tried to reach his parents. The hospital finally treated him, and his parents came in just about the time we were ready to leave. I always have known our most valuable assets are our children. I was devastated. I was responsible for hurting someone. I had to put the Pinto wagon in the shop and borrow Daddy's car to drive to work. Trials are tough, but God is faithful.

On Tuesday, November 12, 1974, Uncle Clifford passed away. I was working midnight to eight. I was sleeping, and my parent's phone was ringing for a long time. This was in the days of a ten-party line. About the time I was going to pick it up, it stopped ringing and started ringing my number. I answered the phone, and it was Wamer, and he asked, "What is wrong with Uncle Clifford?" Mama picked up her phone and blurted out, "He is dead in your front yard." He was trimming a bush on the ditch bank and had a heart attack and died.

Sometime in the spring of 1975, I sold my mobile home and moved to Stony Creek, Virginia. The Carter and Jean Rose Gill extended family became part of my extended family. They became a major part of my circle of friends. Grandma Gill (Elizabeth) was always bringing neighborhood children to church. She visited her daughter in California and flew a suit across the country to see if I could wear it. Calvin Gill had crippling arthritis real bad. I spent many hours talking to him. I lived next door to Carol Williams, Jean Rose's father. He always had a beautiful garden. People would stop by the road and look at his garden, and I always thought they would look at my yard and say, "His grass sure needs cutting."

Flash forward to Mr. William's funeral, I was pastor of his Church, Shiloh Baptist; I said, "I would love to have been his dog he loved and cared for him so." Carter and Jean Rose have three children: Roger, Jeanie, and Henry. As with my younger cousin, who had grown up, I tried to be a big brother to them. I taught them in Sunday School. Carter ran Gill Equipment Company in Stony Creek and farmed. Jean Rose was the bookkeeper for Gill Equipment Company. I would go to the office or the farm whenever I had time from work. They helped me out of my depression. There was always someone to talk to and something to do.

On May 18, 1975, I preached my first sermon. Two weeks before, a man had brought a message and read seemingly every word, and it was the worst sermon I had heard. God dealt with me vividly during that service. I wanted to preach more than ever. "God, I really believe I could do this good. The people are listening to him. I believe they would listen to me. God, what would I say?" God gave me my first sermon illustration that morning. At the end of the service, the chairman of the deacons asked me to preach in two weeks. I asked God for two things in that service. "God, don't let me look too bad, but while I am in that pulpit, let me know if this is really where you want me, and please don't let my nose run."

When I would get nervous, my nose ran constantly. My nose did not run, and I felt at home in the pulpit. Mrs. Florence Winfield came by the door and shook my hand and said that I sounded like Billy Graham. I knew that it was not that good, but I took it as a great compliment. Billy Graham was my favorite evangelist. I had taken a Billy Graham evangelist class in Emporia for the movie *Time to Run*. I attended every showing of the film, driving from Richmond for some viewings to counsel people who came forward at the end of the movie. I shared the Gospel with twenty-two people there in the theater.

I had preached one sermon, and I just knew everything was ready for me to become a preacher. I went to our association director, Reverend Charles Spain, and told him I knew God had called me to preach. I wanted to know what were man's requirements. He said to go to college to get a degree and to go to seminary. It seemed like it was impossible. I had tried for two years to save and was about as financially behind as ever. I had sold most of all my possessions (color television, stereo, mobile home, more expensive cars, etc.), and I had cashed in my life insurance policy. I needed clothes, dental work, and a car that would run. I was a "C" student in high school who had failed English twice. I had asked God to show me what to do in this meeting. It had not turned out as I had wanted.

Pauline Kennedy asked me what it would take for me to go to college. I told her I needed money. She gave it to me. I believed I had to at least look into the possibility of college. One of my high school English teachers, Mrs. Dorothy Ricketts, had become a guidance counselor at Richard Bland College. Before I could hardly get seated, she had me signed up for college boards and summer classes. I completed two classes that summer. I made an "A" in both classes. The last migraine headache I have had was the day of my New Testament exam. I was unable to continue in college that fall because of finances. I went back to work for Wheat First Securities part-time. I worked two jobs for six months.

Barry McGee was the bass player for the Hopper Brothers and Connie when I first met them. Barry and his wife, Donna, became my friends. Soon after I met the Hopper Brothers and Connie, Barry left the group and joined Shekinah. My first gospel music promotion was promoting Shekinah. I would schedule two or three concerts for a weekend, and they would come up and sing. The group members were Johnny Armstrong, Lenny Stadler, Leroy Butler, and Barry McGee. Lenny Stadler had a moving testimony.

One weekend that they were in the Stony Creek area, over one hundred people walked the aisle dedicating and rededicating their lives to Christ. On April 23, 1976, I testified and preached at one of their concerts at the Sappony Ruritan Club, Stony Creek, Virginia. Shekinah disbanded. Johnny Armstrong started a group with his brother, sister, and others; the group name was Southern Cross. I promoted them in the Stony Creek area. Johnny wanted me to testify and speak with the group.

In May 1977, I went down to Madison, North Carolina, and went out with Southern Cross on their tour bus. We went to North Wilkesboro, North Carolina, for a service and had another service somewhere out from Madison. I was supposed to go with them to Myrtle Beach to a campground for a weekend of singing and preaching. It worked out so I could not go with them. Johnny had a stroke at Myrtle Beach. He never recovered and soon passed away. These were great friends. Life has taken us on separate journeys for the cause of Christ, but I will always cherish the memories of our serving Christ together at this time in our lives.

Chapter 23

Answered Prayer

For a year and a half, I waited to get back into college. I prayed, "Lord, if it is Your will, lay it upon someone's heart to help as it seemed that I could not provide the way for myself." As George Mueller's book teaches, I told no one of my prayers. Reverend James Edmonds was the pastor of Sharon United Methodist Church. He reached out to me during my trials of 1974. He had a good singing voice. He did gospel concerts. Under his leadership, I switched my membership back to Sharon. He said I could get more help through the Methodist Conference to become a Pastor.

I celebrated the Bi-centennial of our nation on July 4, 1976, going to see the Hopper Brothers and Connie. It was a blessed day. In October 1976, I went to a concert by the Hopper Brothers and Connie. I had seen on the schedule that they were going to be in an afternoon service in Suffolk, Virginia, soon. I had planned to ask Claude if he wanted me to find a night service in our area. Before I could ask about him about coming to the area, Claude said he wanted to come to the church I was attending. I said I thought it would be ok, but they had not had a gospel sing. Sharon United Methodist agreed to have them sing.

On November 7, 1976, the group came to Sharon. At the end of the service, Claude asked the congregation to be seated. My heart dropped. I had not heard Claude browbeat a congregation into coming forward. I had heard other people do it, but I was thinking this is not going over here. Instead, Claude announced that the Lord had laid me on his heart, and the Hopper Brothers and Connie were going to help me through college and seminary. Connie later shared that the first time Claude mentioned helping me, he could not remember my name. Claude stated the group would pay half of my tuition and Connie, and he would pay the other half. He set up a fund in my name with John and Pauline Kennedy as trustees. My prayers had been answered.

Chapter 24
Richard Bland College, College Beginning

In January 1977, I started back to college, taking a night class in English 101. I was wary of the class because I had failed English in eighth and tenth grades in high school. I made a "B" in the class that was a real encouragement.

Sharon United Methodist was on the Sussex Charge with Fort Grove United Methodist. In the spring of 1977, the Sussex Charge voted for me to go into the Methodist ministry. I had taken my first formal step toward the ministry. I left Media General and became a Huff-Cook Mutual Burial agent. In the summer, I took English 102 and made an "A". I finally received an "A" in English. Miracles never cease.

Mrs. Dorothy Ricketts was preparing to go to Union Theological Seminary in Richmond. She was still a counselor at Richard Bland. She took me to the United Methodist Petersburg District office to meet the District Superintendent. I started Richard Bland full time in the fall of 1977. The selling burial insurance was not my cup of tea, but it provided some income, and it got me back in school full time.

I took twelve credit hours and received a 4.0 my first semester. I started praying about where to transfer. Richard Bland is a junior college a branch of William and Mary. Nothing was happening to move me forward into the United Methodist ministry. Reverend James Edmonds had moved to another pastorate. I went back to talk to Reverend Charles Spain. He welcomed me back as a Baptist, and I rejoined Sappony. Reverend Spain started scheduling me as a supply pastor. I started preaching regularly. I applied to Averett College in Danville, Virginia.

I begin to plan my second semester around Averett College. Averett College was a Southern Baptist College and had a Christian Studies degree. I was not the best mutual burial insurance salesman.

I acquired a job at Virginia State University as a computer operator. My second semester at Richard Bland, I took twelve credits and received a 3.75. I received a "B" in English 204. Professor Paul Smith was a professor of history, philosophy, and religion. I had taken a New Testament class, History 101, and History 102 that he taught. He was a minister. I studied in the library before I would go to work. He taught me how to use the library in my ministry effectively. He found out I was taking summer classes and wanted me to take his Old Testament class. I told him I was going to Averett, and I was going to wait and take it there. I was going to take two classes first semester of Summer School. I thought the Old Testament would require too much reading for me with another class. He looked the class up in the Averett college catalog, and he said his class was the same as theirs, and I should take it. I pre-registered for another class.

The first day of classes, Professor Smith met me and informed me the class I registered for did not make (have enough students enrolled to make a class) and to come on to his class, and I could change my registration after class. I made A's in both classes. I am thankful for my Richard Bland College years. All the professors were helpful. I was blessed to have Mrs. Dorothy Ricketts as a counselor and professors like Professor Patsy Newman, Dr. Joel Whitten, Jr., and Professor Paul Smith that took a personal interest in you.

Chapter 25

Onward to Averett College

June 4, 1978, on the church's 205th Homecoming, Sappony Baptist Church licensed me to preach. After almost five years of trials and prayers, I had completed forty-two credit hours of college and my first formal step into the ministry of our Lord Jesus Christ as a Baptist minister.

I quit my job at Virginia State University, stored my furniture, and stayed with my parents on weekends. I started at Averett College in the fall of 1978. I had a second-floor apartment on North Main. I took Spanish on a pass-fail option. There was a one-credit hour class Ministry as a Vocation that was pass-fail. I could not find a job compatible with my class schedule. After a few weeks, I became discouraged and called home and said I was quitting and coming home.

Pauline Kennedy gave Carol Toone money to drive to Danville and talk me into staying. I came back to the apartment from class, and there were Daddy and Mama sitting on the front porch. They never went into my apartment. Daddy said we would help you stay in college. I said, "Yes sir," and they got back in the car and drove home one hundred and twenty-five miles. I received a check from Claude and Connie Hopper. Carter Gill said he would pay me to sit at the office doing peanut harvesting on Saturdays. I hung out there all those years for free; they should have charged me. Reverend Charles Spain had a place for me to preach on weekends when I would come back to Comans Well each weekend. Needless to say, I stayed and finished the semester.

I carried fourteen credit hours this semester. I received three "A's" in the classes I received grades. Toward Christmas, Reverend Spain sent me to Claremont Baptist Church to preach. I preached at four different churches. I preached the same Christmas sermon four times. Carol would meet me at the church I was preaching or on the way to the church. Daddy asked her, "Had hearing the same sermon four times helped her?" She said, "No." New Year's Eve 1979 was on Sunday. Reverend Spain sent me to Claremont Baptist Church. I preached my first Watch Night Service that night.

Who is this Carol that I keep talking about? I do not remember the exact date, but the Hopper Brothers and Connie were at High Hills Baptist Church, Jarratt, Virginia. I got there early, and I found a seat. Someone asked me would I save a seat for someone, and I agreed. The church was packed. This woman comes in, followed by what seemed like a dozen children, and comes and sits by me. My first thought was that these people know me here, and I hope that they do not think this woman with all these children is with me. The woman was Carol Toone (flash forward Carol Mayes). Carol was a friend of John and Pauline Kennedy. I began seeing her and talking to her at sings regularly. One Sunday night, I was standing on the porch of Readville Baptist Church at Sussex, Virginia, Carol's oldest daughter (a high school student) told me I should date her mother. I thought about it for a while and decided it was a good idea.

In January 1979, I took two sociology classes in the January term at Averett. I received two "B's". I was called as Interim Pastor of Claremont Baptist Church. It was a three-hour drive one way to Danville, Virginia, from Claremont, Virginia. They wanted me to stay in the parsonage on weekends. They had Sunday Night Services. I moved into the parsonage and had a late-night ride or early morning ride to Danville each weekend.

On Tuesday, February 27, 1979, I decided to drive down to Madison, North Carolina, to tell Claude and Connie the good news about becoming Interim Pastor. I had good news, but Connie had bad news. She had found a lump in her right breast and had been to the doctor that day. She had had pains and weakness for some time. The doctor was scheduling a biopsy. We went to Ellisboro Baptist

Church and had prayer. I prayed for her healing, as we all did. I went to see her later in the hospital after surgery. She cheered me up. After twenty-one tests, there was no sign of cancer. God is faithful.

The highlight in the spring of 1979 at the Claremont Baptist Church was the Easter Sunrise Service. We had a community Easter Sunrise Service that started just before sunrise. We had the service on a bluff overlooking the James River up from Jamestown across from the mouth of the Chickahominy River. The James River is wide there. The sunrise was beautiful, coming up and shining across the river. It is good I had just about finished the message, for everyone's attention was on the beauty of the sunrise that reminded us of our Risen Savior. Lee Chilton was the bass singer for the Hopper Brothers and Connie when I met them. He was from Danville, Virginia.

The highlight of going to Averett in my second semester was finding and going to Lee's Father's church on Wednesday nights. I was able to see Lee and hear him play the steel guitar. His Father always brought a good message. I took thirteen credit hours this semester. I did not do as well as I had the first semester. I received three "B's" and a pass on my Spanish Class. I had been happier because I had a pastorate and some income. On the way back to Claremont, at the end of the semester, I stopped and talked to Mrs. Dorothy Ricketts. She was living in Emporia. I was concerned about Averett teaching classes on every other year bases since I was a transfer student; my schedule was not working out. It was going to take an extra year to get my degree in Christian Studies. I was changing majors to sociology. I had a long drive every week. She suggested going to Virginia State University. I could get my degree in sociology and my Christian Studies in seminary. I applied to Virginia Stare University and was accepted. I could commute from Claremont.

Chapter 26

Ordained to Preach

Sappony Baptist Church ordained me to preach on May 27, 1979. Claremont Baptist Church voted to call me as pastor on the same day to coincide with the ordination. Reverend John Crocker was pastor of Sappony and helped me with the ordination process. Roy Lewis, Jr. was the organist. Carol Toone was the pianist. Prelude was by Roy Lewis, Jr., and Carol Toone. Sappony Baptist Church Choir sang the call to worship *Come Holy Ghost.* The invocation was by Gordon Lewis. The Congregation sang, *Where He Leads Me.* Reverend John Crocker did the welcome and statement of purpose. The Youth of Claremont Baptist Church sang *Jesus, Savior.* Jean Rose Gill read the scripture Reading, 1 Peter 5:1–11. Hazel Martin sang a solo, *To the Ends of the Earth.* Reverend Charles Spain gave the charge to the candidate. Reverend John Crocker gave the charge to the church. Pauline Kennedy sang a solo, *He Touched Me.* All ordained pastors and deacons present participated in the laying on of hands. Reverend John Crocker said the ordination prayer. Russell Lewis made a presentation of the Bible. Betsy Nicholson sang a solo, *My Task* John Kennedy said the benediction. The congregation gave the hand of fellowship. Postlude was by Roy Lewis Jr. and Carol Toone. The ushers were Henry Gill and Roger Gill. Five and half years had passed since that night of my attending my first Hopper Brothers and Connie concert, and I felt called to preach. I had completed seventy-five credit hours in college.

I had forty-five credit hours to go. May 27, 1979, was a red-letter day. I was ordained to the work of the Gospel Ministry. I was called to be Pastor of Claremont Baptist Church.

God has been faithful.

This is a picture I had taken after ordination.

Chapter 27

The Claremont Years

I was asked to do a wedding immediately. I was authorized by the Circuit Court of the County of Sussex to celebrate the rites of marriage in the Commonwealth of Virginia on May 30, 1979. I had a home wedding and a church wedding in June. In the summers from Memorial Day until Labor Day, the preachers of Claremont United Methodist Church and Claremont Baptist Church would rotate preaching at Guilford Heights, a beach community on the James River. I performed my first baptism in the James River at Guilford Heights. My sister Pattie Mae Upton and my nephews Walter and Ted Jr. were the first three I baptized. Pattie Mae belonged to Sharon United Methodist in Comans Well but joined Claremont Baptist. The boys accepted Christ as their Lord and Savior and followed through with baptism.

In the fall of 1979, I started at Virginia State University. I did not lose a credit in the two transfers. Dr. Taylor was assigned as my student advisor. He was the head of the sociology department. He was a minister. He taught some of my sociology classes. He guided me through my year and a half at Virginia State University. In the summer of 1980, I took classes through Virginia State University at Fort Lee, Virginia. I completed my requirements for my Bachelor of Arts degree in December 1980. I graduated on May 24, 1981. I graduated Magna Cum Laude.

While at Claremont, I continued to promote gospel music. The Dixie Melody Boys came to sing at the church. The Alphus LeFevre singers came to sing at the church twice. This was when I met Karen Peck, Mike LeFevre, and Scott LeFevre. Huff-Cook would sponsor a group to sing at a church. They sponsored The Nobleman to sing at the church. This is when I meet Danny Parker and Ivan Parker.

In the spring of 1980, we celebrated the twentieth anniversary of the organizing of Claremont Baptist Church. Reverend Ron Wade, a former pastor, came and brought the message. The Seekers were our guest singers for the afternoon service.

In the fall of 1980, the subject of seminary kept coming up. I began to pray for the Lord to give me guidance as to how I should continue my education. I went to talk to Dr. Taylor about entering a master's program in sociology. I thought a master's degree in sociology would enhance my skills in helping people. The Southeastern Baptist Theological Seminary was three hours away. Virginia State University was an easy commute. Dr. Taylor stated that if I was going to stay in the ministry, why was I going to fool around in other fields? I should enter seminary as soon as possible. God places His hand of guidance on the people that surround you. Dr. Taylor was a mentor while I was a student at Virginia State University. God has been faithful.

There were many trials in the spring of 1981. I went back to work as a third-shift supervisor for Computer Science Corporation at Fort Lee, Virginia. I wanted to supplement my salary and prepare to go to seminary. My body did not like working at night and rebelled. Carol and I broke up, and it left a void in my life. I was getting back into my neurotic self. I was working nights and seeing less of people. I was trying to be a good pastor. In March, I went down to look over the campus of Southeastern Baptist Theological Seminary at Wake Forrest, North Carolina. When I drove up on the campus, I had a feeling that this is where God wanted me. As a teenager, I had helped my uncles move Reverend R. D. Patterson from Wake Forrest to Stony Creek, Virginia. He lived across the street from the campus. I had a strong interest in the seminary then. I talked to Dr. Fred Sandusky, the registrar, and he advised me to apply for January. He stated that if it became possible for me to come earlier that he would move up my registration. I applied and was accepted.

I resigned from Claremont Baptist Church. I stored my furniture and moved back with my parents. I continued to work for the Computer Science Corporation through the summer.

Chapter 28

Onward to Southeastern Baptist Theological Seminary

I had prayed for several signs on whether to start seminary in September or wait. I had made no arrangements for a room because I felt if God opened the door for me to go in September, He would have a place for me to stay. On Friday, before classes were to start on Thursday, I had an answer to prayer to start. On Monday, I drove to Wake Forrest to find that there was no reason I could not come, but Dr. Sandusky was in a meeting. He would call me for final approval. There were no rooms available in the dormitory. I tried to find a place to stay, but I was unable to find a living space. I went home discouraged. Monday night, I did not receive a call from Dr. Sandusky. I went to work at midnight. Tuesday, since the answer to prayer had been so positive on Friday, I took a leap of faith and resigned from my job. I went home to wait. I received a call from Dr. Sandusky saying I could start Thursday. He said he had not been able to get a long-distance call to me on Monday night. He had tried. I drove down Thursday morning to orientation. Thursday night, I found an efficiency apartment across the street from the Seminary.

After I had resigned from the Church at Claremont, Mr. Spain started assigning me places to preach as a supply pastor. I begin to look for a job in the Wake Forest and Raleigh area in computer operations. During the first semester, I interviewed with a company in Wake Forest. I told them I would not take a church, but I would stay with them through the years in seminary. When I got the callback, they said it came down to a flip of a coin, and they went with the other person. I finished my first semester.

I had enough living expenses money to start the next semester, but I had to have an income more than supply preaching. I decided to start back the second semester and go until you could withdraw without academic penalty. The Hopper Brothers and Connie were in concert at Pikeville, North Carolina, on a Thursday night. Pikeville is approximately seventy miles from Wake Forest. I prayed about going. I had not seen the group for a while, and I really wanted to go. I did not know if I should burn the gas or not. Even if you had a supply place to preach, you never knew what the church would give you.

Wake Forest was one hundred fifteen miles from Comans Well. I went to see the Hoppers. As I was leaving to go back to Wake Forest, Debra and Roger Talley gave me a check. It was more than an average supply fee from a church. God is faithful. After the second semester started, I was called by Shiloh Baptist Church, Carson, Virginia, to supply preach a Sunday.

Right before the end of withdrawing, without academic penalty deadline, I had an interview in Raleigh in computer operations. I came home for the weekend, feeling I was going to get a job offer in Raleigh the first of the week. I had a call from the Pulpit Committee of Shiloh Baptist Church to become Interim Pastor. The committee had already scheduled someone to preach a trial sermon in the near future. I decided that I wanted to pastor, even if it was not a job offer as pastor. It would get me through the semester. I called and withdrew my name from consideration at the job in Raleigh. I became Interim Pastor of Shiloh Baptist Church in the spring of 1982.

The Sunday the gentleman came to preach his trial sermon, I was invited to preach a revival at Adams Grove Baptist Church. The Monday night after revival services, I was on the way back to Wake Forest listening to the NCCA Championship game when Michael Jordan made his infamous shot, winning the game for the North Carolina Tar Heels. It was a good week for me. We had a good revival at Adams Grove. The Tar Heels had won. Shiloh did not hire the man who had tried out. Before the end of the semester, they called me as their full-time pastor. I moved into the parsonage at the end of the semester.

Chapter 29

"Spirit of the Shenandoah" Campmeeting

I went to Watermelon Park at Berryville, Virginia, for the first time in 1974. It became a goal to go every year. I missed some years. One year I went and slept on the pickup seat of John and Pauline Kennedy's pickup camper. One year I carried a tent. Carol carried her camper for her and the children. Carol and the children went home for the week of the singing to work. She said I could use the camper if I wanted to while they were gone. I thanked her and said my tent would do fine.

One night we had a bad thunderstorm. I woke up and took everything off of the tent floor and placed them on the extra cot I had and laid back down. Before long, I noticed the tent floor was floating on water. I moved into Carol's vacant camper for the rest of the night. I decided that if I could only afford to stay one night, I was going to come one night and stay in a motel.

One year I sold my Stony Creek High School class ring and Smithdeal-Massey class ring to stay in a motel. In 1979, I stayed in an Econo Lodge in Winchester, Virginia. I had a room with two double beds. Tim Bullins, of the anchormen, was a teenager at the time and caught a truck up to the park. He needed a place to stay and stayed with me. Every year was a blessing. I met so many nice people. I was able to share my faith and was fed by the activities of the week. We had Bible Study in the morning, preaching in the afternoon, and gospel singing at night. I would help out wherever I could. I sold and checked tickets. I helped with the youth Bible Study. I worked in the office.

In 1982, at the Tenth Annual Camp meeting, I preached the Sunday morning service. I had never preached a service that had more than a hundred people in attendance. It was an honor to walk out on the stage at Watermelon Park and proclaim the Word of God. The Spirit of the Shenandoah Camp meeting was a great evangelistic effort. Many people were saved and baptized through the ministry of this event over the years.

This is a picture of The Hopper Brothers and Connie taken at Watermelon Park. This is a picture of the group that came to Sharon United Methodist Church.

Chapter 30

How Did I Get Here?

The summer of 1982 was an active one. I settled into my new home and began a full-time ministry. We had morning and night worship services—Sunday School, church training, Royal Ambassadors, Girls in Actions, Acteens, and Woman's Missionary Union. We had an active youth group. We had four softball teams. We had men's, women's, youth's, and children's softball teams. We had Vacation Bible School each summer. I had left a plastic stool on the screened-in porch, thinking I would prop my feet on when I sat on the porch. With all the activities, I seldom had time to sit on the porch. The stool became a receiving table. I would have pies, rolls, food, or an Easter basket at various times on the stool when I would get home.

Soon after I moved into the parsonage, the church gave me pounding. A pounding for those who do not know is a party welcoming the new pastor. Gifts of food, household items, and money are given to the new pastor. My pounding included a survivor kit. There were various gifts in the survivor kit, including a gift certificate for hair growth. Rogaine had not been invented. I was not able to find the place to cash in on the gift certificate. I sure could use it now.

The summer came to an end. It was time to start back to seminary. Shiloh was one hundred twenty-one miles from Southeastern. I drove on Tuesday and Thursday to class for three years. It was just under a two-hour drive. A Master of Divinity is a three-year degree. It took me four years to complete the three-year degree. I graduated from Southeastern.

Baptist Theological Seminary on May 4, 1985. God is faithful. I had answered the call to preach in 1974. It had seemed to be impossible. I had made it. Do not sell God short of what He can do through His people in your life.

Train a child in the way he should go, and when he is old he will not turn from it.

(Proverbs 22:6 KJV)

When I was small, Mama would read me the Bible stories from a Bible storybook. My parents took me to church. I begin to read the Bible for myself when I learned to read. My Grandma Mayes gave me my first Bible on December 25, 1957. As a teenager, on Sunday morning before going to church, I would watch a gospel music television show. I remembered two groups from that show. The Happy Goodmans and a group of brothers who sang with a woman playing the piano were featured regularly. I really liked the group of brothers and the lady piano player who they let sing some. From the album cover of The Hopper Brothers and Connie entitled *TV Favorites* recorded in the 1960s, I quote:

> To work with the Hopper Brothers & Connie is a joy. They have appeared on many television programs, besides their weekly appearance as host on *Inspiration Time,* viewed by millions each week over much of the Eastern United States. As Master of Ceremonies for *Inspiration Time,* I can see why they are so successful. Their Christian fellowship, brotherly love, and willingness to do anything anytime to improve the program so that you, the viewer, might enjoy it more, is evident at every recording session. Their warmth and feeling of a gospel song are evident every time they sing. This album of TV Favorites is just that; songs with the feeling that the Hopper Brothers and Connie put into every song they sing. I know it will be a blessing to you just as it is for me. So until we can join you again in your home through television, remember, "When You Pray, Pray for Us."
>
> —Tom Bodenhamer[72]

---

[72] Bodenharmer, T. (n.d.). The Hopper Brother & Connie TV Favorites. Greenville, SC: Mark Five. Back Cover.

114

I had forgotten their name. I tried to have Kay Lewis to change their name in the church bulletin to Harper. I thought she had spelled it wrong. I came across some old albums in the basement of the Hopper office in about 1990, and they gave me a few. This is how I have a copy of "TV Favorites". To me, it has been like they stepped out of television into my life. Claude, Connie, and the group kept their commitment to me all those years. They paid my tuition to college and seminary. I received grants and student loans that helped with the tuition. They were always there, with their part cheering and praying me on. I quoted, "train a child in the way he should go," what if I had been watching cartoons on Sunday morning and never fell in love with gospel music, God's Music?

I cannot begin to name all the people who helped me through my college and seminary. John and Pauline Kennedy were always there to help. They were the trustees for the fund that Claude set up for my college expenses. Roger and Debra Talley supported me. Sappony Baptist Church took an offering every fifth Sunday for me. Claremont, Shiloh, and all the churches I supplied while I was in college and seminary supported me.

Sharon United Methodist Church members are like members of my family; they supported me. Fort Grove United Methodist Church supported me. Guilford Heights Beach Service took an offering for me. Ralph Owen would send me money for textbooks. My extended family supported me. Carol supported me. My mother made patchwork bed quilt tops and sold them and gave me the money. I thank everyone who prayed and were a part of this miracle in my life. Thank God for the miracles that He worked through His people for a saved sinner like me.

Chapter 31

Quotes from Claude Hopper

An excerpt from *After All These Years: The Authorized Biography of America's Favorite Family of Gospel Music, The Hoppers:*

Learning To Give

We make a living by what we get; we make a life by what we give.— Winston Churchill

Sometimes God sends special individuals or circumstances our way for a purpose. Perhaps it is to get our attention or to teach us important principles. Christians walking sensitively in His light often recognize the fingerprint of the Almighty in unusual occurrences.

Through a series of circumstances, after singing at Sappony Baptist Church, in Stony Creek, Virginia, Claude and Connie felt led to do something out of the ordinary in making a financial commitment to help a young man complete college and go on to seminary.

"It was the fall of 1976, and to be honest, although we were certain we were being led to assist this fellow, we were concerned about the magnitude of such a commitment. We sensed the Lord's prodding in this as never before. The tuition was a phenomenal amount of money for us, but we began to pray and trust," Claude said. "and we turned the college fund commitment over to Christ."

It was amazing that in future weeks, God blessed the ministry in ways that made the ongoing assistance possible. Donations from the Lord's people increased at concert dates over the following months, and Claude and Connie could see exactly what was happening: the Lord was meeting the need and teaching them something new.

After our commitment, then friends from Sappony Baptist Church began giving to this young man's college fund, as well, God really blessed.

"The Lord led us into a deeper relationship with Him by giving to this young man," Claude recalled. It was at this point, the group came to recognize it's really impossible to receive the Lord's entire blessing if you don't give generously and cheerfully to His work.

This fellow, named Hugh Mayes, entered Richard Bland College on a full-time basis by September. On June 4, 1978, during the 205th Homecoming at Sappony Baptist Church, Hugh was licensed to preach.

"Hugh became a pastor; we were thrilled," Claude said. On July 26, 1981, he was invited to proclaim God's Word at Watermelon Park. It was a wonderful experience for the Hoppers and for Hugh and a glorious culmination of the group's yielding to the Lord's desire for them to give abundantly.

This is How God Works

"Sadly, as the years went by, we lost contact with Hugh. However, one day he just popped in at our office in Madison. It was a wonderful moment to see him again and to hear what the Lord was doing in his life," Claude said.

Coincidentally, around that same time period, we had just invested in a computer, Claude said. "Hugh asked us what we were doing it?" I explained, "Nothing really. We don't know how to use it yet."

As they came to find out, besides being a pastor, Hugh was also a gifted computer programmer. As he examined the new hardware and got a feel for what the Hoppers' special needs were, he offered to set up a workstation and program the computer. He would also train the staff on how to use his customized software.

For a while, Hugh traveled to the Hopper office one day a week as he developed various programs and backup systems to modernize and transform the Hopper organization.

"Hugh set up systems and methods that helped save us time in many areas of the ministry and developed an extensive royalty program for our publishing company."

Every now and then, he still drops by the Madison office to update the various programs and visit the family.

"It's a God thing," Claude concluded. "This is how the Lord works, in that the Hoppers made a small gesture many years ago, but God just keeps giving, giving, and giving back to us. The Lord has given everything back to us hundreds of times over. It taught us a vital lesson giving: you just can't out-give the Lord!"[73]

[73] Davis, K. F. (2006). All These Years: *The Authorized Biography of the Hoppers* (First Edition). Woodland Press, LLC.

Chapter 32

No More School

For someone at five years old who said I am not going to school, I spent twenty-two years completing twenty-one years of school. I was thirty-seven when I finished Southeastern Baptist Theological Seminary. Let's back up a year to 1984. Shiloh Church celebrated 100 hundred years of worship in the sanctuary with a homecoming on September 30, 1984. Reverend Jack Partain was the guest speaker for the morning service. Mr. Fred Anderson of the Virginia Baptist Historical Society portrayed Dr. William Hatcher at the afternoon service.

Shiloh had celebrated 125th Anniversary on October 22, 1961, with Dr. Sydnor L. Stealey, President of Southeastern Baptist Theological Seminary, as the guest speaker. On May 25, 1986, Shiloh celebrated our 150th Anniversary. For our Sesquicentennial morning service, we had Dr. W. Randall Lolley, President of Southeastern Baptist Theological Seminary. For the service, I grew a beard and rented a suit to look like a pastor of the late 1800s. The Petersburg Railroad Company built a railroad station across the road from the church. The land was deeded on July 21, 1891. The Portsmouth Baptist Association held its 101st session at Shiloh Baptist Church. Many of the delegates came by train. Halifax road is the old railroad bed. The American Legion had a truck built like a train. We had Dr. Lolley, members of families with four generations, and I ride in on the American Legion train to the church on the old railroad bed to re-enact the Portsmouth Baptist Association meeting. Many were dressed in period attire.

In one of my classes, I learned that it was healthy to have a hobby. I decided to model railroads. The parsonage had a full basement. I had plenty of room for a layout. I was by the phone if someone needed me. This was before the day of cell phones. I built a 28ft by

12ft by 2ft layout with two 4ft by 8ft tables in the middle for train yards. I made electric blocks in the track so I could switch power on and off to a section of the track. The engines and rolling stock were HO scale (1:87 scale). I built buildings and landscaped the layout. Many hours went into the layout. It did relieve stress.

Shiloh had a no-sell policy at the church. I did not invite groups in because of their dependence on product sales for support. The Gospel Melody singers from Madison, North Carolina, did come to the church and the surrounding area several times. The Hoppers were in Richmond on Saturday night and at Sappony Baptist Church on Sunday afternoon. They came and stayed at the parsonage. They sang several songs without setting up the equipment for the Sunday morning worship service. Watermelon Park flooded, and The Hoppers moved their camp meeting to Pikesteam, West Virginia. I went for a couple of days in 1986. In 1987, a group of RA's went for several days.

Shands Road intersects with Halifax Road on the right side of the church property. One night I was awakened by a noise. I looked out of the bedroom window, and I saw a car that did not negotiate the turn into Shands Road. A police car was sitting behind the car. I decided that the people in the car had help, so I went back to sleep. At about five a.m., the doorbell rang. It was the police checking to see if I was alright. Three robbers had wrecked and ran. I went back to bed to be awoken later by the police. They wanted me to unlock the educational building so they could search it. I watched them search the building, expecting to hear gunfire at any moment. There was evidence someone had been in the building, but it was empty. The yard was full of State and County Police cars. They finally caught the robbers. It was not a usual night at home in Carson.

This is a picture of Carol. Shiloh had met its goal. A goal of Shiloh was to get their bachelor preacher a wife. The survival kit that the church gave me had a list of all the single women in the church, from the babies to the oldest single lady member. I conducted a funeral and shook hands with the family, and stood off to the side when Mrs. Essie Lee came up and pointed out an attractive woman. She had good taste. I appointed her chairman of the pastor's wife search committee.

One summer night in 1986, I got a craving for ice cream. I decided to drive into Colonial Heights to a Friendly's. I had never done this. On the way to Colonial Heights, I started to think about Carol so strong that I almost stopped at a phone booth and called her. We had broken up in the spring of 1981. This was a little over five years later. When I walked into Friendly's, Carol and her sister were sitting at the first table. Carol asked did I want to sit with them. I did. Jerry Clower was going to be at the state fair in Richmond, Virginia. I had seen him in a Chapel Service at Southeastern Baptist Theological Seminary. I thought going to see him would be a good first date to start our relationship again. She said no. I was discouraged, but I called her again.

Christmas of 1986, we were engaged. I had a very busy December. I had multiple funerals and hospital visits and activities at church. My Aunt Frances Mayes died. Scheduling time with Carol was limited. She was off work on a Friday; I decided to ask her to go to Richmond to Clover Leaf Mall with me. She said yes. My intention was to take her to lunch and ask her to marry me doing lunch at Piccadilly's and if she said yes, pick out a diamond.

At lunch, a couple I knew came and sat at a table near us, Mr. and Mrs. Roy Cain. I lost my nerve to ask her to marry me at lunch. My time was limited because of all my commitments. I could not come back to Richmond another day before Christmas. I had to ask her. Romantically, I steered her to the ring case in J. C. Penney's, and I ask, "Do you think we need one of these?" as I pointed to the diamonds. She said yes. I did not buy a ring in Penney's, but I got a thankful yes. She picked out a ring at another store, and I purchased it. I wanted to give her the ring on Christmas Eve. Our family got together on Christmas Eve. I wanted them to see the ring. Mama told us how pretty Sharon United Methodist Church was, and we should go and see the Christmas decorations. We went to the church, and I gave her the ring in church.

My Aunt Edith Lewis was at a nursing home near Shiloh. We were to take her back to save Mama and Daddy, a seventeen-mile trip. Aunt Edith could not get in the back seat comfortably. Carol got in the back seat. We are romantics!

Carol met the approval of the pastor's wife search committee. She came to play the piano for Shiloh in the summer of 1987. We were married on August 28, 1987. We were married on Friday. Reverend Charles Spain performed the ceremony. We went to Natural Bridge, Virginia, for Friday night.

We came back to the parsonage on Saturday, and I preached Sunday. Shiloh gave us a shower and farewell party Sunday afternoon. We were given access to a cottage at Nags Head, but we did not stay because I had so much to do in packing to move to Virgilina, Virginia. My uncles had farm trucks, and we loaded my furniture and trains on two trucks and moved the following Thursday. Carol found a job in South Boston, Virginia. She only had to stay at her home for two weeks and commute to Virgilina on weekends. Within a week, we got married, said goodbye to one Church family, and moved to start a new ministry with a new Church family. I preached the next Sunday Morning, September 6, 1987, at North Fork Baptist Church.

Chapter 33
Years at North Fork Baptist Church

The newlyweds moved to Virgilina, Virginia. North Fork welcomed us with open arms. They gave us a pounding soon after we arrived. I had preached a trial sermon for the North Fork Pastor Search Committee at Hitesburg Baptist Church, a few miles from North Fork Baptist Church. They had suggested I ride by North Fork and see the church and parsonage. I was a happy individual when I saw that the parsonage had a basement. My trains had a home. Later that fall, North Fork members helped us move Carol's furniture from her house. Carol and I settled into our new home together.

Soon after we arrived at North Fork, a young man, Tyler Hudson, went to volunteer and then to work for Habitat for Humanity. I believe the year was 1988. Habitat was sponsoring a walk down the Eastern seaboard. Tyler was on the Pastor Search Committee that hired me and knew I was from the Petersburg, Emporia area. They needed a coordinator for the area. We would meet the walkers in the afternoon and plan the walk to a place to stay overnight. We would plan the next morning's walk. We would have three rest stops, dinner, breakfast, and lunch for the walkers. After dinner, we would have a program for the walkers and the community to help tell about Habitat for Humanity. I accepted the challenge. Richard Bland College opened its doors to us. The walkers stayed in the gym. The Hopper Brothers and Connie came and sang for our program. We fed lunch in Emporia in Veterans Memorial Park.

I was more active on the Dan River Association. I was Mission Committee Chairman for several years. The association had a fair booth at the Halifax County Fair in South Boston, Virginia. I made a four feet by eight feet train layout. I had a picture of a train engine on a blue paper entitled Heaven Bound and a picture of a train engine on red paper entitled Hell Bound. We had a table in front of the layout with free water and gospel tracts. A picture and an article were published in the Baptist state paper *The Religious Herald*. This display had a very positive witness. I had people come up under conviction to talk about salvation. One night toward the end of the week, the building seemed to be empty. The main stage had someone performing; a man came up to the table saying he was from the dark side and performed a rap. The scary part was that in the rap, he guessed my age. It was very uncomfortable.

The association sponsored a missions team through the Virginia Baptist Association to Tanzania. We sponsored a missions trip to Monterey, Virginia, in Highland County. We held Revival Services and helped build a basketball court at Highland Baptist Church. I preached two Services.

I asked one of the young teenage ladies what the church could do for her. She said, "Sponsor a women's softball team." We did. I coached. We did not win a game in the first year. The second-year we won some. We won a second-place trophy in a tournament. The women gave me the trophy. We did not have a team the next year. North Fork had a lot of youth. The area churches had Fifth Sunday Night Sings together. We had a group of girls that sang, The Free Spirits. Dean Hopper sold me a Peavey amplifier, microphones, and two used speakers. The Free Spirits were ready to travel locally. We later had a group of boys, The Red Bank Revival. We also had a group of younger girls that used the PA system. I cannot sing. I am a prison singer behind bars searching for a key. I enjoyed running the PA for these young people to sing gospel music.

North Fork sent delegates to the Baptist Association of Virginia Annual Meetings. I rode the train from Greensboro, North Carolina, to San Antonio, Texas, to the only Southern Baptist Convention I have attended.

Claude Hopper stated at the Habitat for Humanity sing at Richard Bland College that they had a personal computer. I had worked on mainframe computers in the 1970s, but I had not worked on a PC. Sometime after the singing, I went down to Madison, North Carolina, to take a look at their computer. I asked Joyce Hopper how to turn it on. On the mainframe computers, if you did not turn on in sequence, you could cause a problem. This was the start of working in the Hopper office part-time. I wrote an accounting system for them, a mailing list program, and a royalty program. Virgilina is eighty-two miles from Madison. It was not too long a trip. I was able to help at the Singing at Brown Summit, North Carolina, and also the sings at Eden, North Carolina. I edited, compiled, and typeset Connie Hopper's book *Heart of the Matter*. I enjoyed the days of working in the office with Joyce Hopper and being able to see the Hoppers regularly.

Sherry and David Tuck is a young couple I performed a wedding for. They had a baby with multiple disabilities. I organized two benefit sings featuring The Hoppers. We donated the funds to The Clinton Tuck Fund to help with their expenses. Clinton's life was just a few years, but he was a Blessing of God's.

One of the Blessings at North Fork was the young people we had in church. I was privileged to baptize fifteen young people in a service. This is still the biggest baptism I have performed.

While we were living in Virgilina, Aunt Edith died on March 31, 1989. She had been a great inspiration for me. She taught Sunday School and an avid supporter of our family. She helped me in becoming a teacher in Sunday School. She had kept Uncle Clifford's car. Mama would drive for her when she wanted to go somewhere. If I needed a car, she would always let me borrow it. The first Sunday I preached at Shiloh, I stop at the mini-mart, and my car would not start. I called Mama; she and Daddy brought me Aunt Edith's car. I was on the way to church.

Carol and I were at North Fork for six years. Our parents were aging and began to need our support. I resigned from the church in October 1993. We have fond memories of the years at North Fork, and now, twenty-five years later, we still have many friends from North Fork on Facebook and from Virgilina.

Chapter 34

Visual Foxpro Programming

What started out as a favor for Claude became a job. I started programming with Dbase4 and worked my way into FoxPro and Visual FoxPro. I stopped by Woody's Chevrolet in Stony Creek, Virginia. Woody Oakley is a member of Shiloh Baptist Church and brother to my Aunt Violet Lewis. Woody asked how the church was doing and what I had been doing lately? I filled him in on how we were doing at North Fork and told him I had bought a computer and was helping the Hoppers. Woody said he needed help that Reynolds and Reynolds were phasing out its accounting program for the TC1000. I looked at the input data and the accounting book Reynolds and Reynolds supplied and wrote a Dbase4 program to produce the accounting in Chevrolet account numbers to submit to Chevrolet monthly. This was still while I was at North Fork. I had an income to supplement my church salary.

I bought a mobile home and put it on the lot in Comans Well, Virginia. I used it for an office and a place to stay. Virgilina is a hundred miles from Comans Well. Holidays when we would visit our parents from Virgilina, we had never spent the night. Carol would stay with her mother and stepfather every other Friday night to see the children and grandchildren. With call forwarding on the telephone, we could spend the night in Comans Well and still be in touch with the church family.

I did not have a set day off from the church but considered it my day off when I would go to the Hoppers or Comans Well. I continually updated the program until I reached Visual FoxPro. Alton Owen bought Woody's Chevrolet. He owned Owen Ford in Jarratt, Virginia. I took the accounting program and modified it with Ford account numbers. When I resigned from the church, we moved into the mobile home, and I continued to use one bedroom as the office. I stored my trains.

I began to supply preach on the Petersburg Baptist Association again. We began to attend Sappony Baptist Church on the Sundays I was not preaching. I was elected a deacon. I became Chairman of the Deacons.

I continued to write software. I wrote a Chrysler accounting program, a car finance program, a funeral home program, town water billing program, town office, and payroll program. I wrote an item auction sale program and a livestock auction for Gray Auctions. I wrote a livestock auction program for Southside Livestock Market in 1995. Since 2000, I have contract worked for Southside Livestock Market on Wednesdays and processed their accounting. I worked part-time for The Bank of Southside, Virginia. I did the night processing on the mainframe computer. I began to work days for the Bank writing reports on a PC computer, accessing the mainframe data using IBM Cognos Impromptu.

In the Spring of 1994, when Carol and I came home from church, Daddy said that Mr. Lynwood Bobbitt wanted to see me. Daddy and Lynwood had been friends for a lifetime. Lynwood was four years older than Daddy. Daddy and Lynwood would help each other out on the farm. When I was growing up, while Mama and Sally Bobbitt would be cleaning the Sharon United Methodist Church, I would look through the old records of the church. If I saw a Sunday that Lynwood and Sally missed before they were married, I would ask where they were. She would just snicker. I can, in my mind's eye, see her sitting in the choir at Sharon snickering when something funny was said or happened. Daddy and Lynwood always worked together threshing peanuts. When I was big enough to help, I would help Lynwood with stacking the peanut vines. Lynwood was living at their daughter's Betsy Nicholson at the time. Carol and I went down to Betsy's home to see Lynwood. Lynwood asked me to do his funeral at Sharon United Methodist Church. If the current preacher did not want me to do the funeral, he told me how to get him unassigned from the church for a day. Lynwood died on April 18, 1994. I helped carry the casket into the church. I stumbled going up the steps. Bobby Owen looked at me and said, "I can see him laughing at you." I used the United Methodist *The Book of Worship* for the service.

The year of 1995 was another stressful year. I was writing the software for Southside Livestock Market. I was in the testing mode of running parallels getting out the garbage. I learned the phrase in the computer field early on in the 1960s "Garbage in, garbage out." Mama was in the hospital for thirteen days with gallbladder surgery. A gallstone had blocked the duct. It had killed the gallbladder. She had an infection. She had a reaction to morphine. We were beginning to think we were going to lose her.

She recovered. Sandra Dodson, who worked for the Stockyard, fell off a tractor and was ran over by a disc. The Stockyard wanted to start using the program. I really was not ready. During the first sale, the program locked up and would not run a buy invoice. I had written the program so that if the checks did not match the buy invoices, it would not print a bill. One of the buyers asked me, "Who is going to pay my truck driver while you are fixing the program?" I broke out in a sweat, sitting in front of the air conditioner. I removed the safety in the program, and we completed the sale. Mrs. Carolyn Baber, who owned the Stockyard at the time, looked at the reports for balancing before I did and said we are out of balance. I asked how much, and she said ten cents. I offered to give her ten cents.

Walter Upton, my nephew, was killed in a car accident in July 1995. Daddy died on September 30, 1995. Daddy was given back health-wise; he was eighty-three. Uncle Bob and Aunt Helen came from Richmond to see him and Mama on September 29. When they left, I asked him, didn't he want me to buy a calf at the stockyard for him to take care of? He said no that he was worn out. When Carol came home from work, we went out to eat. When we got home from eating, there was a car in the yard of the parsonage. I walked over to the parsonage to see what was happening. Woody and Catherine Dunn were there. Mama woke Daddy up from a nap. He would not eat supper (dinner). He was not hungry; he had eaten with Walter over at the Optimist ball field. She could not convince him he had not eaten with Walter, who had died in July. After Woody and Catherine left, he finally ate something and went to walk the dog. The last clear words I heard Daddy say were, "Marse, it's bad to get old and doddie," (Daddy's expression for an old tree that has decay and is dying.) as he talked for Spot. I went home—about 5:00 a.m., Mama called me to come over, she said there is something wrong with your Daddy. I called Wamer, my brother, who was on the Waverly Rescue Squad to come to check Daddy out. We called Pattie Upton, my sister, to come. We started calling the extended family. Daddy died at home that afternoon. We had a stressful year, but God has been faithful.

This is the last Lewis Mayes extended family taken before Daddy died. I wrote this soon after Daddy's death.

The Day Daddy Went Home

Daddy was a simple man, a peanut farmer,
Life for him was work, friends, family, and Jesus.
The twinkle in his eye made your heart grow fonder
Of life as Daddy taught us to follow Jesus.

One fall day, Daddy started his long journey home.
The doctor had told us that his heart was worn out.
He said he had a good life and was going home.
It was not a time for us to fret or to pout.

Daddy's naps had grown closer and longer each day.
We thought that he was having his usual nodding.
When he awoke, he said he had been to supper,
With his grandson who had already made the crossing.

That night as he prepared to walk his dog Spot
Often Daddy talked for Spot I hear him say,
"Marse, it's bad to get old and doddie."
These were the last earthly words I heard Daddy say.

I can imagine him saying a little later.
"Master, itis bad to get old and doddie.
I haven't been able to keep the pace lately.
I am tired and weak; it's so good to be home."

And the Master replies, "You have fought a good fight,
You have finished your course, You have kept the faith.
Here's your new body, here put on your robe and crown,
I have the best cure for being old and doddie."

In the fall of 2000, they took the over counter medicine off the market that I was taking for my allergies. I had not been to a doctor since moving back from Virgilina. Dr. Walker was nearing retirement. I decided to go to a younger doctor. I went to Dr. Hall Squire. I had taken out a life insurance policy while living in Virgilina. They did a blood test, and my enzymes were high. I convinced them it was probably due to the over counter medicine I was taking. The blood test that Dr. Squire took showed that I had Hepatitis C. "Hepatitis C—Over 3 million Americans are infected with the stealth virus. This potentially lethal virus is now four times as widespread as HIV. It was not discovered until 1988."[74] I had Hepatitis C for over thirty years, since 1968. I was infected from a blood transfusion. The first article I read called Hepatitis C, the silent killer. I had a liver biopsy. It showed that I had inflammation of the liver, and I had fibrosis of the liver. I needed treatment. The medicine was estimated at $25,000. I did not have the money. It was not covered by insurance because the medicine was given as out-patient. A friend of Carol's recommended that I go to VCU-MCV to see Dr. Stravitz. He directed me to a drug test program conducted by Dr. Mitchell L. Shiffman, sponsored by Ribapharm, Inc. The monitoring and drugs during the test were free. I was healed and declared virus free. On November 4, 2005, I sponsored a "Praise God For Healing Gospel Sing" featuring Nathan Potts, Cindy Coghill, Highway to Heaven, and Down East Boys. I thank God for using infected blood to save my life in 1968 and providing the healing from that infection in 2004. I thank God for Jesus' perfect, precious blood that He shed on the cross for a sinner such as me.

---

[74] Cowley, Geoffrey. 2002. "Hepatitis C: The Insidious Spread Of A Killer Virus." *Newsweek.*

Chapter 35

Shiloh Baptist Church Fire

While Shiloh has experienced some challenges in its past, perhaps one of the most momentous moments was the destruction of the education building due to a fire. On August 17, 2002, a bolt of lightning struck a tree and traveled down the tree to the propane tank. The lightning traveled down the gas line in the center of the building and caused a massive explosion. Flames reached up to 100 feet in the air, and the Carson Volunteer Fire Department (CVFD) worked tirelessly to extinguish the flames, but the building was destroyed. Thanks to the hard work of the CVFD, they were able to prevent the fire from spreading to the sanctuary. Everything in the education building was destroyed, but the spirit of Shiloh could not be destroyed.

In order for Sunday School to continue, a trailer was brought in that housed three classes. The office and storage area at the rear of the sanctuary was transformed to serve as a nursery and children's classroom. Local churches made donations of Sunday School materials, basic supplies, and library books to replace what had been destroyed by the fire.

On February 2, 2003, Shiloh broke ground on a new educational building. In order to keep the rebuilding costs low, church members donated countless hours volunteering their services wherever possible, from cutting boards to painting walls and even preparing meals for hungry workers; there was no shortage of hard workers. The members of Shiloh Church rallied together, proving the old saying that a church is not just a building, but it is the people.

All the hard work culminated on February 1, 2004, when the dedication for the new educational building was held. The new educational building did not just replace what was lost but provided additional space for Sunday School classrooms, an updated kitchen, and a large meeting/social room. Shiloh is very thankful that the educational building was able to be rebuilt without incurring any debt. At the dedication, church members, community members, and local churches were recognized for their contributions made during the rebuilding at Shiloh. Whether it was a monetary donation or the donation of supplies, cabinets, furniture, or time the outpouring of love that was displayed was paramount.[75]

---

[75] "Notes on the History of Shiloh Baptist Church: 125th Anniversary, 1975." n.d.

Chapter 36

Recycled Pastor

Eighteen years to the weekend, August 25, 2005, Shiloh Baptist Church called me to supply preach for a Sunday. They called me as interim pastor and later as pastor. I have entered my fourteenth year as pastor. I have performed weddings in the 1980s and saw their children born. I have performed the children's weddings and saw their children born. I have known six generations of some families. Carol has played the piano and directed the choir since the fall of 2005. The church family is our family. I thank God for each week we have together.

Shiloh celebrated its 175th anniversary on June 11, 2011. Fred Anderson, executive director of the Virginia Baptist Historical Society of the Center for Baptist Heritage and Studies, presented a portrayal of Dr. William Hatcher during the morning worship service. Lunch was served in the fellowship hall after the service.

Chapter 37

Our Trails

Mama had cataract surgery. You are not supposed to bend over or stand on a ladder or anything after surgery. I went over to check on her the next day, and she was standing on a step stool cleaning a kitchen cabinet. I asked her, "What are you doing?" She replied, "I am cleaning the cabinet. It's dirty. I couldn't see the dirt before." I took the step stool home with me and called Aunt Maggie Lou Lewis to come and sit with her.

Mama began having mini-strokes. She got so she could not write with her right hand. The doctor prescribed physical therapy. She did not want to go, but I took her. She was walking with a walker, so I parked at the door long enough to get her in the building and went to park the car. When I walked in, she said she had told them she did not need therapy; she was ready to go. I did her writing after that, but she worked her hand until she was able to sew again. I went over on December 23, 2003, night to check on Mama. She seemed a little more confused than usual. I went back on Christmas Eve morning before I went to work at The Bank of Southside, Virginia. She was getting things ready for our family Christmas Eve Supper. We were going to have it at Sharon United Methodist Church fellowship hall. She was fixing little things of cookies for the great-grandchildren. She was fixing for a family reunion. I received a call around 10:00 a.m. that Dorothy had found Mama unresponsive. The neighbors had called the rescue squad. I left the bank and met the rescue squad, and followed it to the hospital. When they took her into the emergency room, I followed. I told them no heroics that she wanted it that way. She died on Christmas Day morning. She had her family reunion with a different part of the family.

Carol had been slowing down physically. She decided to go to Virginia Cardiovascular Specialist for a series of tests in the spring of 2010. It was near Krispy Kreme Doughnuts, so I decided to go to get doughnuts and coffee while she had the tests. The doughnuts were great, but Carol's tests were aborted because of her low heart rate. She was waiting for me when I returned. They gave her a heart monitor to wear for a couple of days. When the monitor was read, she was called to come to Saint Mary's hospital right away to have a pacemaker implanted.

In the Fall of 2010, Wamer had an aneurysm in his abdomen to rupture. He was in the hospital for thirty-nine days. I went to see him often. He was on the respirator some of the time and could not communicate. On Wednesday morning, November 17, 2010, I received a call that he was dying to come to the hospital. I tried to start my car, and I could not get the key in the ignition. I called Uncle Roy, and he sent Chucky to help me. Chucky could not get it to work. He took me to Uncle Roy, and I borrowed his car and went to the hospital. Through the ordeal, I communicated with the family at the hospital; they thought I was not going to get there before he passed away. When I did get there, I went in and told him I was here and said it was ok to go on. I had told him earlier not to leave me here with these two sisters. Within a few minutes, the alarms of the respirator sounded. He died.

Carol had four grown children when we were married. She had a son, Michael, and three daughters Theresa, Sheryl, and Karen. Theresa and Michael both had heart problems. Theresa died in June 2011 and Michael in July 2011, less than a month apart. Losing two children in less than a month has been a trial.

The year 2013 was a busy year for the doctors and the hospitals. In the early Spring, Carol had driven to work, she called me and said she had made an appointment with a doctor at Virginia Urology at Stony Point, Richmond, Virginia. Kidney stones were no strangers to Carol. Throughout our married life, there have been many lithotripsy procedures and appointments with Dr. Feminella. This time was different. She had walked into the hospital to work; they pushed her out in a wheelchair. We arrived at the appointment, and they said she definitely had kidney stones. She was on a blood thinner, so they were going to wait several days before they treated her to get her off the blood thinner. I told the nurse I didn't understand that she had walked into work and now could hardly stand up. She told that to the doctor, and he recommended going to the emergency room at Saint Mary's hospital.

Leaving the building, the automatic doors would open for you to get out, but would not open for you to get back in. I had left her just outside the reach of the automatic door opening. Carol was in a wheelchair, and I was beginning to think she did not have strength enough to get the chair to where the door would open, but she finally did. When we got to Saint Mary's, while we were waiting in the waiting room, Carol could not hold her head up. I sat beside her, holding the back of her head. I had a cold, and I was coughing. People who could were moving away from us and others were going to get a breathing mask. They found that she had a kidney stone blocking a tube and that she had sepsis. Dr. Charles A. Seabury came in and did a procedure at around 1:30 a.m., placing a stent in to allow draining until she passed the kidney stone. Carol was in intensive care for five days. Later that spring, they removed her gallbladder. This was extremely painful because Krispy Kreme Doughnuts is near St. Mary's Hospital, and I stop to get doughnuts on the way to her doctor's visit. The first visit, I stopped and brought the doughnuts to the car, and the smell made her nauseated. The next trip, I did not want to make her nauseated, so I ate the doughnuts inside. She still got nauseated from the smell of my breath. She stayed nauseated and could not eat for six weeks. She was forced to retire from Southside Regional Hospital. She has walked with a walker ever since. She had kidney stones blasted at Johnston Willis and Retreat for the Sick. In August 2014, Carol had a lipoma thirteen inches long removed from her right thigh.

Chapter 38

A Trip to Goodlettsvile, Tennessee

Friday, September 19, 2014, Promiseland Quartet, LeFevre Quartet, and Karen Peck and New River recorded videos in Goodlettsville, Tennessee. I rented a van. Nathan drove down to meet the group on Thursday. Shari, Simone, Tristan, Carol, and I went to the recording. This was my third experience of being at video recordings. I had been at a Hopper recording in Brown Summit, North Carolina. I had been at the recording of videos for The Harvesters, Brian Free and Assurance, and Ivan Parker in Sanford, North Carolina. Carol, Nathan and, I went to Sanford. Nathan and Shari and the children went into Nashville on Friday morning, Carol and I stayed at the motel. On Saturday, Nathan left with Promiseland for more sings and on to the National Quartet Convention. We came home. Going down, Simone and I had sat on the third seat of the van, and she about talked me to death. Shari and I alternated driving back home.

On October 24, 2014, I promoted Ernie Hasse and Signature Sound and Promisedland Quartet for the third time. The first year we were at Hopewell High School, Hopewell, Virginia. The second-year, we were at Mount Pleasant Baptist Church, Colonial Heights, Virginia. This year we were at West End Baptist Church, Petersburg, Virginia.

Chapter 39

Meant to Give Help Ended Up Needing Help

On Saturday, November 8, 2014, we were going by Shiloh Baptist Church to pick up Carol's notebook with her choir notes and go into Petersburg shopping for a few items at the drugstore. I unlocked the door and went into the church and picked up the notebook, and came out and locked the door. As I was walking to the car, a young man was coming towards me. I spoke to him, and he spoke and asked, "Is the church opened for prayer?" My answer was, "No, but it can be."

He and I proceeded to the door, and I unlocked it and went in. We went into the sanctuary and prayed. I asked him, "Where do you live?" His reply was nowhere. He looked to be in his early teens. He and I went into the church office and talked. He had not eaten, so I said Carol and I would take him out to eat. While we were at the restaurant, I called the Prince George Dispatcher and asked if there was any place to take him to stay. I knew there was a homeless shelter in Petersburg. We decided to put him in a motel until Monday. He said he would go to church on Sunday, but it did not work out.

I took him out to eat Sunday afternoon. Monday, I drove him to Prince George Social Services. They referred me to District 19 in Prince George. Here I finished piecing together his story. He had cut his wrist at Virginia Beach. Someone had seen him and called the police. A judge ordered him treatment at Popular Springs Hospital in Petersburg. Upon release, he had no place to go, and they took him to the Petersburg Homeless Shelter. He walked the railroad tracks and ended up on Halifax Road and to Shiloh Baptist Church. District 19 called Popular Springs and received a report of his treatment at Popular Springs. He was supposed to have medication. He said he threw it away. He did not want to go back to the Petersburg Homeless Shelter. Prince George District 19 told us about the intake place for Richmond Catholic Commonwealth Charities on Grace Street. We went to the intake center. He could not get a place to stay for the night, but they told us a place to go for his medicines.

It was late, so I took him back to the motel. Tuesday, when we got to the Richmond Behavior Health Authority to try to get his medicine, it was closed for Veterans Day. I decided to go to VCU-MCV and try to get his medications. They called Popular Springs Hospital to find out the medication prescribed and reissued and filled the prescriptions. They said he had an appointment with District 19 Petersburg on Friday. I took him back to the motel.

On Wednesday, I went by and picked him up and took him to the stockyard as I went to work. As people from the church, stockyard, and our family found out about his situation, people gave clothes and money. I was able to keep him in the motel and give him money for food. I drove him to District 19 and went in to listen to the counselors as they talked to him. He came to church on November 16, 2014. I continued checking out possibilities for places to live cheaply. On November 18, 2014, we went to the Social Security Office to apply for disability insurance. They needed a report from his counselor from his teen years. I went and got the report. He worked a few days for Steve Brockwell, one of our church members.

He was on medication, and things seem to be going well. Carol asked, "We cannot afford to continue keeping him in a motel. Why don't we bring him home?" On November 25, 2014, we let the young man move into our house. Things through the holidays and into the New Year went well. In February 2015, he started to work for Starbucks at the Davis Travel Plaza, Stony Creek, Virginia. I would take him to work and get him after each shift. When I was not able to take him, someone would step up to make sure he was able to get to work or back.

April 5, 2015, was an Easter Sunday to remember. Shiloh and Carson United Methodist Church have Easter Sunrise Service together. I preached the service. The young man had to work and got off at 3:00 a.m. on Easter Sunday morning. I had to get up and get him from work. I had to be at Church by 7:00 a.m. Carol and the young man were coming to church in time for Sunday School. After Sunrise Service, we have breakfast at the Carson Ruritan Clubhouse. I started back home to pick Carol and the young man up, and my car breaks down. I call home for them to drive Carol's car, and the car won't start. It had not been driven in so long the battery was dead. We had to call a neighbor, Milton Dunn, to come and start the car. Blake Gilliam came for me and drove me to the church.

Steve Brockwell and extended family saw the need for the young man to have a car. Steve has a car lot and financed the young man a car. The young man had walked up to church with only the clothes on his back. He had a car to drive, a place to stay rent free, clothes, an iPhone, and a community that was helping him.

On May 15, 2015, the young man came home and asked if I could spot him $20 he wanted to meet a girl for a movie in Colonial Heights. He said he had his paycheck in the car and could pay me back later. I gave him $40. He had been coming in late and promised he would be home early. He did not come home all night.

I went to Verizon to get a list of his phone activity. I finally got the girl on the phone, and she said she did not meet him. I continuously called and texted him from 3:00 a.m. Saturday morning until late Saturday night. He would not answer the phone and only texted back a few times.

I drove up and down Emerald Road, looking for him multi times. I walked the paths off Emerald Road. I began to get a suicidal text from him. "The demon has told me to follow it tonight, so goodbye Hugh." "Nothing can help me anymore. I need to be alone. I've tried praying. It only makes it mad. Hugh, I'm sorry you don't understand, I need to be alone. Please stop calling me. I'm not going to change my mind. It's for the best. You don't need to get people to call me. I'm not coming home."

I went to Sussex Courthouse and before a magistrate to see if the police could find him. His phone went dead. Sunday, I did not hear from him all day and decided he must be dead. We went to a gospel sing in Richmond to see the Hoppers. Carol and I got home, and I got a phone call from VCU-MCV that he was in the hospital. He had cut his wrist and somehow ended up in the James River.

On Monday, Carol had an appointment with the cardiologist. I left her there and went to visit the young man. He was as out of it as I ever have seen anyone. He was seeing a demon in the corner of the room. I asked him why he would not look and talk to me. He said because the demon was standing next to me. I said if I moved to the other side, would he look at me and talk to me? He said yes, and he did. He had a sitter in the room watching him. He had to go to the bathroom. The sitter stood at the door with it open. I had to get the car keys from hospital security. He did not know where he had left the car.

I left and went back to pick up Carol. I went to a police station to ask where he was picked up and where to look for the car. They were very helpful, and I found the car right away. Carol followed me in my car as I drove his car to a friend's business in Richmond to park it. There was evidence of drugs and alcohol use in his car. Mack Gilliam went with me to get the car back to Carson. When the hospital was ready to release him, I asked that they place him in a place for some help. I told them that we would not let him come back to our house. They released him to the street. They made an appointment with District 19 in Petersburg for that Friday afternoon. District 19 let him go too. I checked him into a motel again. The search for a place to live was on again. Memorial Day was spent looking for a place.

By this time, the young man was working in the west end of Richmond. On Saturday, June 6, I went to the door of the motel, and he would not come to the door. I had told him I would be there to go look at an apartment in Hopewell. I called him, and he did not answer the phone. I went to the manager and had him come with a passkey to enter the room. The night latch was on the door. All I could think was he was trying suicide again.

The manager went to the next room and tried calling him on the motel phone. He did not answer. I was asking the manager was there any way of cutting the chain, when he came and opened the door. He had been paid the night before, and for the second time, he had blown his entire paycheck. I told him I could not support him or ask other people to support him anymore. The motel was paid until Wednesday, and that was all the help he was getting from me. The phone was in my name. I cut it off on Sunday after he made threats, trying to make me continue helping him. On Monday, I called District 19 and asked them to contact him and help him. They called me back and told me the things he wanted from our house. I put them together and took them to the District 19 office in Petersburg. I asked how he was doing, and they said they could no longer talk to me because of the laws. It was his request.

Sunday, June 14, Carol and I went to Richmond to see the Down East Boys. We went to eat after the concert with Carol Lawson, Rachel Lawson, and the Down East Boys. We got home after 1:00 a.m. Around 5:30 a.m., Carol was screaming at the young man, and it awakened me. I just stood up when he came around the foot of the bed and pushed me back against my desk and stabbed me twice. He stabbed me in the center of my chest and right above my heart. I could hear Carol talking to the dispatcher. He picked up my wallet, car keys, and went running back to the den. He did not even bring his own knife. He used one of our kitchen knives. It is hard to find a knife in our house now. He collapsed my lung and just did not make it into the heart cavity. I sat down for a few seconds as I could hear the air escaping from my lung. I got up and ran to the back door to see him getting into my car. He had stabbed Carol five times in the neck. She was in the recliner in the den when he broke in, and he jumped on her and stabbed her. She was to leave for Florida for vacation on Wednesday; he knew she had her vacation money in the house. He took it. I called our neighbors Louise and Stanley Benson and told them we needed help. I did not know if we would pass out before the rescue squad came. They came over and stayed with us until the rescue squad arrived and looked after the cat and house until we returned home. We were airlifted to VCU-MCV. Her helicopter landed on the roof first, and mine last. I was wheeled past her helicopter and into the emergency room. They sewed Carol up on the roof with no anesthesia. Carol was taken into surgery. She was on the respirator for several days. We were admitted to the trauma unit of the hospital. Carol's code name was Gardener, and my code name was Hair Streak.

While I was in the emergency room, they did a CAT scan. They came and told me that Carol was going to surgery. I asked for my phone. I called the young man's adopted mother to tell her what had happened. I called Buddy Darby, our Chairman of Deacons. I called Tammy Roark of Southside Livestock Market. I called our daughter Karen and my sister Pat. A doctor walked up to the bed and said, you are mighty calm. I told him I was a minister, and God had us in His Hands. When the young man ran around the bed, an inaudible voice said to me, "You are not going to die today." I had a chest tube inserted to inflate my lung. My oxygen level would not stabilize.

They began to run tests. I begin to feel like Job. Every time a new doctor came into the room, he or she brought more bad news. I was diagnosed that I have intermittent dysphagia and Schatzki esophageal ring. Dr. Gabor Bagameri walked in, asked me, "Do you know what an aneurysm is?" I said, "Yes, my brother died with one." I was diagnosed with an aortic aneurysm. I had a hole in my heart that had been there since birth. I told the doctors that I wanted to go home for three days. I was walking the halls as well as ever. I had work to do.

My grandson brought the laptop to the trauma unit. The stockyard called the hours into me. I set the payroll up to print checks. I gave Nathan instructions on how to print checks. He went to Blackstone and printed the checks. I had a report for Packers and Stockyard that needed to be completed, and I needed to go home. If I died before I got back to the hospital, I knew where I was going. They began making preparations for me to go home with oxygen, but they found the hole in my heart. Dr. Zachary M. Gertz did a cauterization and implanted an Amplatzer Cribriform Occluder in my heart. My oxygen level went immediately up. I came home the next day. I had been living for almost sixty-seven years with an oxygen level that they would not let me out of the trauma unit with. They found that I had plaque in my carotid arteries. It was not enough to operate yet. I made follow-up appointments for all the other diagnoses. There was some good news while I was in the hospital. Nathan and Shari announced that the results of a pregnancy test that they were going to have a baby.

The young man was captured after a two-day manhunt. He was arrested during a traffic stop in Richmond driving my car. He pled guilty to five felonies. They were two counts of attempted murder, breaking and entering, robbery, and larceny of a motor vehicle. He was sentenced to 100 years with 55 years suspended and 45 years to serve in prison

I was a pumpkin in a first-grade play. I did not want to get my picture taken. What a face? The Coman House is in the background. It is next door to the old parsonage. They tell me I can still get a frowning face. Thank God I have a cure in our Lord Jesus Christ.

Chapter 40

A Summer of Trails and Blessings

Carol had left the hospital a week before I did. She stayed at our daughter Karen's and husband Bob's house in Toano, Virginia. They went back by our house for Carol to get a few things, and there was a group of men from church cutting grass and power washing the house. Steve Brockwell had seen on television news that the house needed power washing, so they power washed the house.

I was in the hospital for thirteen days. On the way home, Carol told me that Ida Ezelle Kitchen had died. Ida had lived in Comans Well most of my life. She had lived in the Taylor house. She had said the house was too cold and drafty and had bought a mobile home and parked it beside the Taylor house. In the later years, I would spend a couple of Sunday afternoons a month visiting her. She would share stories from the past many before I was big enough to remember.

Ida had a pony cart. When Wamer, Dot, and Pat were young, she took them for a ride. Wamer wanted to steer the pony. Ida, Dot, and Pat were sitting on the back of the cart. The pony started to trot; they were on a dirt road. Ida, Dot, and Pat bounced out of the cart. Wamer looked back, he saw they were gone and laid the reins down on the seat, and jumped from the cart. Ida had a pony cart in her later years. She gave many a child rides through the country around Comans Well. She would call me over to hang a curtain or to do a little task. I would wear old clothes around the house that are just about worn out. When she had something for me to do, so I didn't change, I went over in my old clothes. She told me that a preacher should always dress better than that. A few days later, there was a bag hanging on the mailbox with a new pair of jeans. Carol and I were gone, we came home, and a big section of grass had been cut. Ida had ridden her lawnmower over to the house, thinking we were home, she could not walk that far. She decided to cut grass, thinking we would be home soon. We were later coming home. She went home before her gas ran out of the mower. She was in her nineties then. I went shopping for a certain type of jeans for Ida. I have never shopped for clothes for Carol. In May 2015, her mobile home burned just before we went to the hospital. I visited her at a friend's home before we were hospitalized. I was unable to attend the funeral.

When we got home, there was a big box of cards there with several hundred cards. I did not realize it, but we had made the national news. We had cards from around the country. We had cards from prayer groups around the country with individual notes in them. We had been prayed for at the Southern Baptist Convention. Don Crain visited repeatedly and brought us a check to the hospital from the Southern Baptist Conservative of Virginia. We received a letter from Paige Patterson, the President of Southwestern Baptist Theological Seminary. Claude and Connie Hopper called us in the hospital and continually. The day of the stabbing, the hospital waiting room was full of people expressing their concerns and prayers. When we arrived home, people began bringing food to us.

We had made the news multiple times. They had shown the helicopters in the field with the fire and rescue vehicles. There were many vehicles in the yard and field. Church members were interviewed. Nathan Potts, our grandson, was interviewed. We were interviewed at home by Wayne Covil WTVR-TV news. Carol made the statement, "God's hand was on that knife." The story lead was "God's hand was on that knife, Sussex pastor detail recent attacks."

Wayne found out I liked donuts. He drove from Richmond to bring us a box of donuts and pay us a visit with his wife. I was interviewed at church. Singing News in the August 2015 issue of the magazine printed a picture of us with the caption "Pastor Hugh Mayes and his wife Carol of Yale, Virginia, were seriously injured when their home was broken into and they were violently attacked.

The couple is well known by many Southern Gospel artists as they've hosted many in their home and church."

Shiloh set up a *Go Fund Me* page for us. Some people did not give to the *Go Fund Me* page but gave gifts of money to us. People at Southside Livestock Market made a donation. God is surely faithful! His people truly blessed us.

In a few days after I returned home, I was able to finish the report for the Packers and Stockyards, and Lawrence Jarratt, my bus driver when I was in the first grade, drove me to Blackstone to get Clarence Simpson's signature on the report and to fax the report. I must tell the truth, Lawrence was a senior, and I was a junior when he drove the bus. I was privileged to preach Lawrence's ordination service, ordaining him to the Gospel Ministry.

The summer was busy with doctor's appointments. I had dental work that they wanted to be done before the aortic aneurysm surgery. I went to the dental clinic at VCU-MCV. I had to have a liver scan to check my liver because of Hepatitis C. I had to go to a gastrologist to check on the dysphagia and Schatzki esophageal ring. I had appointments with Dr. Bagameri, who kept saying the sooner I had surgery, the better. All these appointments were at VCU-MCV. One July afternoon, I was on the way back from a doctor's appointment, I called Shari. I was going by to see her and Tristan. She was at the hospital. I asked if she needed me to come by, and she said no that her mother was with her. I went to see Lear and Dot Munford. Lear was recovering from a fall. While I was there, Nathan called and said they were going to have twins.

On Thursday, September 17, 2015, three gospel groups united for one cause, a fundraiser to benefit Hugh and Carol Mayes medical fund. The sing was at West End Baptist Church Petersburg, Virginia. The groups were Promisedland Quartet, Anchormen Quartet, and Down East Boys. Two other groups made donations, The Harvesters and The Hoppers. Allen Hunter of The Harvesters attended the concert. Claude Hopper called within fifteen minutes of our getting in the car after the concert to see how the concert went. My only regret is I wished we had had a guest book. People were there from everywhere, showing an outpouring of love and support—People from our past, some I had not seen since high school. It was an awesome night. It was in some ways like a wake, but we were alive to experience it. God showed us His love through His people. God has been faithful.

The Skyline Boys were singing at Dollywood on October 2, 2015. Nathan had joined The Skyline Boys at the first of the year. Carol, Shari, Tristan, and I drove part of the way down to Pigeon Forge, Tennessee, on Thursday and spent the night. On Friday and Saturday nights, we attended the National Quartet Convention. On Saturday, Shari, Tristan, and I went to the Dollywood to see the Skyline Boys. Carol stayed at the motel to rest. We saw the Kingdom Heirs. While they were changing the stage and setting up for the Skyline Boys, Shari, Tristan, and I rode the train through the park. We stayed for two performances of the Skyline Boys. This was my second visit to Dollywood. In October 2010, Carol and I had gone to Dollywood to see the Down East Boys. We were celebrating Carol's twenty-ninth birthday for the xx time. We spent the day in the park. We were some of the first to arrive so Carol could get a handicap scooter. We ate breakfast in the park. We toured Dolly's museum. I took a picture on Dolly's tour bus. We toured the Southern Gospel Music Hall of Fame. We saw the Kingdom Heirs. We attended all three concerts by the Down East Boys. After the concerts, we went out to eat with the Down East Boys.

I was scheduled for aortic aneurysm surgery the week of October 18, 2015. Dr. Bagameri would have performed the surgery and would have gone out of town. He postponed the surgery to October 26, 2015. I had taken off Sunday, October 25. I thought I was going to be in the hospital. The Skyline Boys were in Ivor, Virginia. Carol and I went. I thank Dennis Powers for his prayers and support the day before my surgery. When Dr. Bagameri went to repair the aortic aneurysm, it split in his hand. He implanted a pericardial tissue heart valve (a bovine valve). I remember Dr. Bagameri saying that he had given me fifteen more years and that they should be able to fix any more problems with my heart. The first thing I thought of was Hezekiah, Isaiah 38:1–5. I thank God for using Dr. Bagameri to extend the time of my life, and I thank God for extending my life, for He is the true healer; doctors are His instruments.

I hallucinated on the drugs they gave me for pain. They set me up on the side of the bed; in my mind's vision, they pushed a button, and the bed automatically set me up in a chair. I told them that they could not get the bed back after they had made the bed a chair. I was down near the entrance of the hospital, and the art students of VCU were given a performance. I could see people coming and going to the performance. I thought the friend of the young man who had stabbed us was trying to kill me. Someone had come in and sprayed a blue spray into the ceiling vent. I saw writing on the glass door to the unit. I tried to convince the nurse of the gas in the vent and the writing. Buddy Darby was visiting, and I tried to convince him as well. Have you ever seen your pastor out of it, hallucinating? I hope not. Nathan and Shari came to see me, and they said I did not make sense. Thankfully, it did not last too long, and I got back to my normal craziness. I was in the hospital for eight days.

It was time for the payroll for the stockyard to be completed while I was in the hospital. I had just stopped hallucinating. Nathan went to Blackstone and helped with it. I was able to do the month-end accounting when I got out of the hospital. Nathan and Lawrence were my carriers. I could not drive for six weeks.

I started back preaching. Carol was my chauffeur. My lungs began to fill with fluid. I had fluid drawn several times. They decided that I needed a video-assisted thoracoscopic pleurocentesis. I was to go into the hospital on Monday, December 7, 2015, for the procedure. I preached on the Sunday before. I did not realize how bad I was. Buddy Darby and several others tried to get me to go home; they would cancel morning worship service.

In the afternoon, I begin to feel like I should go to the emergency room, but I kept saying to myself, *you can make it to in the morning.* Uncle Roy drove Carol and me to the hospital. Nathan was working. I was to go in and have the procedure and come home the next morning. I was in the hospital for nine days. The doctor told Carol that I stopped breathing during the procedure. It was a long nine days. They would not give me pain medicine because I had hallucinated before. They put lidocaine patches around my lungs to relieve the pain.

One of the prettiest sunrises I have ever seen was the Sunday morning I was in the hospital. The nurse set a chair where I could sit and look out the window and see the beauty. God is an awesome God with the beauty of His Creation. Thank God for His healing one more time. I remembered that my Uncle Wilson had died three months before I was born with his lungs filling with fluid. This was a delayed result of the stabbing. I kept begging to go home. I had stockyard work to do. The drainage tube just kept draining. They let me go home, and it was almost a week before it stopped draining. Uncle Roy brought me home. When we turned into the driveway, I begin to get mad. Our driveway had been fixed with crush and run. Carol had been after me to have it fixed. I was going to get Uncle Roy and the cousins to fix it with river gravel from their farm. I thought she had gone and spent the money to fix it. I was ready for a good argument when I entered the house, but Shiloh members had had it done. They also said that along with Oakland Baptist Church under the leadership of George Campbell that they were going to build us a ramp for Carol. God continues to bless us through His people.

Tammy Roark called in the payroll for the stockyard on Wednesday night and came to pick up the checks on Thursday morning. She brought us a cheesecake and other gifts from the stockyard. Since I have a bovine valve, she said if I started mooing at the stockyard that they were going to put me in a pen and sell me.

The year 2015 was quite a year. I stood at death's door three times, but God blessed me and kept me alive. God showed me through the young man how His love comes to us through His Son, His Holy Spirit, and His people, the Church. I saw the outpouring of love for a homeless young man. I saw the outpouring of love to an older couple.

Chapter 41

A Better Start But the Doctors Continue

The year 2015 started with Carol having a hip replacement. After this, she had to go for physical therapy. The year 2016 started with Nathan and Shari having twins. The twins were born on February 4, 2016. Isabelle Faye and William Patrick were welcomed into the family. I did not make it to the hospital for the births. When Tristan Riley was born Tuesday, January 22, 2013, Nathan called around noon on Monday said they were on the way to the hospital. I went over to the hospital. They said it would be a while, so I went over to Chesterfield Town Center to visit a friend who had a business in the mall. I came back to the hospital, and it was still going to be a while, so I went out to dinner. Tristan was born in the early hours of the morning. I returned home at 5:30 a.m.

Carol continued to have health problems. She hemorrhaged and ended up in Saint Mary's for blood transfusions. She was on blood thinners. She constantly had problems. After the stabbing, Carol changed to a cardiologist at VCU-MCV, Dr. Kenneth Ellenbogen. He implanted a Watchman device so that she could be taken off blood thinners.

It was time to cut the pampas grass. Theresa had given Carol pampas grass for Mother's Day years before. We planted it on each side of the drive near the road. Since the three hospital visits in 2015, Carol said she did not think I should cut it. I said I was not an invalid, and I was going to do what I can long as I could. The devil tells you can't do things. The thought came to mind that Uncle Clifford had died cutting a small bush on the ditch bank after having a heart attack in prior years. I had had an aneurysm etc. that I was going to end up in the ditch like Uncle Clifford. I told myself I was just paranoid, so I cut the pampas grass. I was cleaning the grass up and lost my balance and fell in the ditch. There I lay like Uncle Clifford, but thankfully

I was able to get up. Wayne Story, our neighbor, cuts our ditch bank when he cuts his for us now.

I started going to the dental school at VCU-MCV for dental work. I have had a twitch on the left side of my face for years. I had an appointment years ago with a neurologist in Franklin, Virginia. He said to quit drinking caffeine, and I could possibly get Botox injections. It was a hard step to take, but I gave up Mountain Dew and started drinking decaf coffee. The twitch has grown worse over the years. I needed dental work on the left side of my face. The dentist would not complete the work without knowing what was causing the twitch and scheduled me for an MRI in August 2016. I have a blood vessel resting on the nerve that controls the muscles of the left side of my face. I have had a TIA, a mini-stroke. I started seeing a neurologist, and I am given Botox injections to relax the muscles to control the twitching every three months. For those of you who like shots, it is fun, five shots around the eye, one at the corner of your nose, and one in the neck. My dental work was completed.

Christmas Eve 2016, Carol fell in the kitchen. We usually have a Christmas Eve Candle Light Service at Church, but for some reason, we did not. We knew all families were finishing up having their Christmas Eve dinner. We called 911. We told them we needed help to get Carol up from the floor, but we did not need the rescue squad. They sent a deputy and a squad member to pick her up from the floor. Carol has fallen five times where we have had to have help to get her up. One time they sent two deputies to help. She had fallen in the yard. We had come through the rain. It was thundering and lightning. I rushed to unlock the door and turned back to see her lying in the yard. I got an umbrella to hold over her. Thankfully, it did not rain. One of the deputies told her, "Mrs. Mayes, you do not have to fall for us to come to see you. Just call us, and we will come."

In August 2017, I had shingles. I went to the emergency room at VCU-MCV. The person at the registration desk picked up on the droop of my lip and that I was having chest area pain; I never sat down and was taken into triage immediately. There was someone on the computer looking up my record while another one started to examine me.

Christmas 2000, I had just received my diagnosis of Hepatitis C. I went to our family Christmas Eve reunion; my niece Sylvia Upton Norris announces she had just been diagnosed with breast cancer. She had surgery at the beginning of 2001. She had a long period of being cancer-free. She was able to see her children grow up. She lost her long battle with cancer on March 17, 2018. She and our daughter Theresa were born on the same day; now, they are together in heaven.

In October 2018, Carol had nine kidneys stones blasted. It was the day of the remnants of a hurricane coming through. We left the Retreat hospital about 7:30 p.m. Tornados had touched down around Richmond. It was raining hard. We did not get on Interstate 95 but took our time on 301. When we got to Stony Creek, there was no electricity. When we got home, we set the alarm off. ADT called before I could find a flashlight to see to turn the alarm off. The aftermath of the stabbing, we burn lights twenty-four hours, seven days a week, and we have ADT security. Carol has posttraumatic stress. If I heard a noise, I would get up and walk through the house. I have fallen out of bed once, trying to get away from an intruder in my dream. Here comes Carol with her walker to help.

Chapter 42

My Gospel Music Career

I have loved music all my life. Since 1973, Southern Gospel Music has been my favorite music. I have one problem. I cannot sing. I have been told that I burn up the wires to the nursery with my singing. I am a prison singer. I am always behind bars looking for a key. I have thought about singing by giving free concerts and charging people to get out. Wendy Bagwell used to say that he asked God to make him a great singer. God said no, but He would send him a crowd that didn't know the difference. God has given us a grandson, who is a great singer. I still cannot sing.

Nathan is the son of our son, Michael. Michael left Taryn before Nathan was born. We did not know that Nathan had been born until he was twelve. Michael had told us about Nathan the summer before and that he was coming to live with him. The first time I met Nathan, we were taking Michael and Paula to a concert featuring The Harvesters and Ivan Parker at Victory Tabernacle in Richmond, Virginia. Nathan was supposed to be at his mother's. We had not bought a ticket for him. At the break in the middle, there was a drawing for CDs. Nathan's was the first name drawn. He won a Harvesters CD. He came back to sit by his Daddy in front of us. I leaned up and asked did he have a cd player. He said he did not, so I told him I would buy him the cassette tape special if he would give me the cd. He asked, "When are you going to get the tapes?" I replied, "Tonight after the concert."

I bought three Harvester tapes. He left the concert saying I want to be a gospel singer. The next time I saw Nathan, he had learned all the songs on the tapes. Earl Brewer had a piano solo on each tape, and Nathan did not know the songs, but he had made-up words for the piano solos. I had the sound system that I used for the youth at Virgilina. I took it to Nathan. We drove him to a Harvester's sing in

167

Mechanicsville, Virginia. He sat up front and sang every word.

I preached at Purdy Baptist Church as a supply pastor. I asked Nathan to sing a special. I knew he could sing, but I didn't know if he would be able to sing in front of people. He did great. Soon after that, we went to a Harvesters Concert, and they called him up to sing on "Wonderful Time". He was thirteen at the time. We went to a Brian Free and Assurance concert; Nathan was sitting in front of me; when asked for a tenor singer, Nathan's hand went up. I started reaching for his hand, but it was too late. They called him on stage to do *Looking for a City*. He did this four times. Nathan was called up to sing by these other groups: The Hoppers, The Dixie Melody Boys, The Kingsmen Quartet, and The Travelers. He started doing solo sets and concerts at sixteen.

The year he graduated from high school in 2008, I took him to NQC in Louisville, Kentucky. We helped with The Down East Boys table that year. He was offered a job with the Northmen and accepted a position as lead singer for Calvary Calls. Nathan has sang with Promisedland Quartet, The Skyline Boys, The Dixie Melody Boys, and the Anchormen. He has filled in for The Down East Boys. While Nathan was with The Dixie Melody Boys in 2019, he had the opportunity to sing on the Main Stage at the National Quartet Convention at the Leconte Center in Pigeon Forge, Tennessee. He formed the Covenant Ground Trio. He sang and managed the Trio for a while.

I promote gospel music. We have had these groups in our church at Shiloh, or I have promoted them in neighboring churches: The Hoppers, The Dixie Melody Boys, The Down East, The Anchormen, The Harvesters, Ernie Haase and Signature Sound, Promisedland Quartet, The Skyline Boys, and Covenant Ground Trio. I have always wanted to travel on a Southern Gospel Music bus and tell people about Jesus. Maybe this book will do it for me.

Chapter 43

Oiling the Squeaking Wheels—God's Grace

Carol and I quote Minnie Pearl's famous saying, "How-DEE! I'm just so proud to be here." We are thankful and grateful for all the blessings God has blessed us with. God has brought us so many things; His Grace has been sufficient.

Carol has had treatment or emergency treatment in Saint Mary's, Saint Francis, Southside Regional, VCU-MCV, Johnston Willis, Retreat, and Sentara Williamsburg, Virginia. Several of these hospitals she has been to multiple times. I believe God is using her as a test dummy. After one CAT scan, the doctor came back and told her she had half a brain. I said, "Amen." While visiting one doctor, Carol was listing all of her aches and pains: the doctor looked at her and said, "I don't know what else to do with you but take you to the woods out back and shoot you." Carol was putting on her makeup to go to see the doctor, and I told her, "Don't put on any makeup. Let the doctor see how bad you really look."

Laughter is the best medicine. Seriously, how many people can say that they had a person jump in her lap while in a recliner and stab her five times in the neck, sewed up on the roof of a hospital with no anesthesia, and all these procedures, lost two grown children within a month, and gets up on Sunday morning walking with a walker to go to church to play the piano and direct the choir. We must praise and thank God because God is faithful.

I have had miracle experiences. The time my lung collapsed at nineteen when I was given blood transfusions and had gone into blood pressure shock. The time I was battling depression and tried to commit suicide. The time The Hoppers said they would help me. It was like they step out of television and into my life. The time Carol and I got back together after a little over five years. The time I had chronic Hepatitis C. The time we were stabbed. The time I had an aortic aneurysm that split in the doctor's hand. The time I stopped breathing during video-assisted thoracoscopic pleurocentesis. The time in the early hours of the morning, I was driving Carol to the hospital. She was in pain from a kidney stone, and she told me to run the stoplight or else. No, that was not really that serious. God's Grace oils this squeaking wheel. We must praise and thank God because God is faithful.

I hope this account of squeaking wheels has caused you to pray and receive the oiling from God's Grace. We all need a touch of His Grace. If you do not know Jesus as your personal Savior, reach out to Him today and make Him the Lord of your life. You are going to spend eternity somewhere... in heaven or hell. I want to see you in heaven.

Chapter 44

A Plea for Help

We need help in the mental health field. When I was young, you were put away in mental institutions and forgotten too easily. The doctor told my mother that she should put my sister, Dorothy, away and forget she ever had her. Dot had had brain damage at birth and was slow developing mental skills. She was mistreated by a first-grade teacher and developed a fear of school and blocked formal education. If Mama had listened to the doctor that day, my sister would have lived her life in an institution. Today we have better mental health care, and it is more accessible. Today, with the HIPAA laws and human rights laws, we let mental illness go untreated, and violence is created. My rights end where yours begin. You or I should not be able to infringe on the other one's rights. When someone has a mental illness, it needs to be treated. My depression needed treatment. I found my treatment through the Word of God and His people.

I tried showing the young man this path because I could identify with his suicide attempts. I realized he needed more help than I could give him. I knocked on the mental health doors, trying to get him help. I had seen him three times, claiming he as his lips moved that he was talking to demons. He would go running. He would come into the house and say that a demon chased him. I prayed with him more than I have ever prayed with anyone in a short period of time. He responded positively while taking his prescribed medicine and even wrote to his brother that he was going to church and starting a new life.

When he got a job and a car, his desire for illegal drugs and alcohol begin to rule his life. The second suicide attempt in about eight months should have been a flag to the mental health system. It should have been a red flag that he needed mental health treatment for his own protection, much less Carol and mine. I had a text from the day he made his second suicide attempt that said that the demon was after him and that he was going to follow the demon. A week before he tried to kill us, I had threats to what I must give him and do for him, and I said, "No!" I never thought he would try to kill me. I called District 19, which is a community health clinic asking for help for him, and they told me they could not talk to me because of HIPAA.

The end result is Carol and I found out how strong our God is. Yes! It has left us with problems, but we are able to thank and praise God. It bothers me that an individual that I had let live in our home and tried to help would try to kill me. At the sentencing fifteen months after the attack, the young man was asked, "Do you have any regrets?" His answer, "Yes, I did not kill him."

This comment hurts more than the stabbing. I used to pray for him daily. As time goes on, I pray for him occasionally, but when I pray, I pray that he will find the Grace, Love, and Peace in our Lord Jesus Christ. Carol and I had forgiven him before we left the hospital. I hope he will receive the Lord and forgive me for whatever caused him to want to kill me. A young man's life has been ruined. So many of the mass shootings and only the Lord knows how many others have been hurt or killed because a person does not get mental health treatment.

There needs to be an outcry for changes in the treatment of mental illness. It is a disease and needs to be treated even if it violates HIPAA or someone's rights. I found out after my aortic aneurysm surgery how drugs could change your state of reality. I experienced depression, and I know what it does to your response to life. I found the Devine Healer, and He is the Best, but we are humans, and God heals us through His people. We need a good mental health field that treats preventively and not let the institution a person ends up being a prison. Are not the young man's rights being violated in prison? His rights could have been violated in treatment and on to a productive life. If I have evidence of a crime, I am called to testify as a witness at a trial. I should be able to be a witness to a mental health agency in reporting a person's mental health.

In January 2019, I received a letter from the young man. He stated how sorry he is for the stabbings and asked for forgiveness. He stated that he was not really his self that he was following evil. He feels God is not through with us. Carol and I forgave him immediately. We are living with the after-effects of the trauma, and it is not easy. I pray this book will be an inspiration to people and lead people to Christ. I do not want to see anyone going down the same path like this young man. The letter was an answer to prayer.

Chapter 45

Challenges

I pray that you have accepted Jesus as your Lord and Savior.

Behold, I stand at the door, and knock: if any man hear my voice, and open the door, I will come in to him, and will sup with him, and he with me.

(Revelation 3:20 KJV)

If you have not let Him into your heart, He is standing knocking. Let Him in. You may say I do not hear Him. You do not hear the television until you go into a room that has one and turn it on. Make yourself available to the Word of God.

I have been a Methodist Church member, and I am a Baptist pastor. God speaks to me regularly through His people, His churches, His Word, and His music. I have been to a Roman Catholic, Pentecostal, Pentecostal Holiness, Church of God, Presbyterian, Christian, Church of the Nazarene, Episcopal, Seventh Day Adventist, and Non-Denominational churches, to name some. I have been to camp meetings, coliseums, services on the river bank, tobacco warehouse, college campuses, high school campuses, baseball fields, home prayer meetings, homes. As long as they are preaching or teaching the Word of God, the Bible, or singing the Word of God through hymns and gospel music and I go looking to meet Jesus, God speaks to me.

We must make ourselves available to hear the Word.

For where two or three are gathered together in my name, there am I in the midst of them.

(Matthew 18:20 KJV)

Have you gathered in Jesus' name lately? I have gone to support the church, support the pastor, support a follow Christian, support gospel singing, and now it is my job as a pastor to go, but our main goal should be to meet Jesus and worship and praise Him. I have hidden under a pew. I went to a gospel sing on July 4, 1976, with my mother. I was feeling very alone in this world, and Connie Hopper worked her way down the church aisle through the chairs of people to tell me that God loved me. I have had Claude Hopper ask a crowd to sit down during an invitation to say the Lord had laid me on his heart to help me through college and seminary. I have been at a service and very distressed about a family member that was having trouble. I would get very emotional when Peg McKamey would sing *God on the Mountain.* Carol and I set about six or seven rows from the front. Peg, not knowing me or my situation, came to the end of the pew and sung *God on the Mountain* as if she was singing it just to me. God is on the mountain, but He comes to us in the valley.

I still work at the Southside Livestock Market. We have more and more people coming to the sales that don't speak English well and do not know how to bid. It is frustrating when they thought they bought the animal for the price per hundred pounds, not the price multiplied out times the weight. After you explain, they start talking in a foreign language. You cannot help them because you do not know what they are saying. God cannot help us if we do not understand what He is saying. Avail yourself to the Bible. Avail yourself to the teaching and preaching of His Word. You can't understand a game until you know the rules. I could not have been on the team that broke a thirty-game losing streak if I had not played basketball. You cannot have the best life possible until you know the rules that are from the Creator Himself. Just talk to Him. He will help you with your problems. Be on God's team.

I try to see lessons in life from God according to my day-to-day life experiences. A Christian's life may be the only Bible some people read. When we sin or have the appearance of sin, people notice. We may be a stumbling block in their life. I wrote a hog marketing program for Joe Gray Auction. He left his computer at the hog barn. He bought the computer and paperwork and left it on the front porch. It was set in the sun for a little while. The paperwork and computer smelled so bad, I could hardly stand bringing it in the office. I wrote a hog buying station computer program for S & J Vallarii Livestock. I went down to Wilson, N. C., to one of their hog buying stations. I did not see a hog. I just worked on the computer in the office. When I got home, I went over to see my toddler great-nephew. I picked him up to hug him. He laid his head on my shoulder and immediately jerked it up. I smelled like a hog. We Christians know that we have forgiveness for sin, but we must live a life that points to Jesus and points away from sin. We should not have the scent of sin.

The Gills lived down the road from me at Stony Creek. Their cows gave me a theological education.

> The ox knows its master, the donkey its owner's manger, but Israel does not know, my people do not understand.

> (Isaiah 1:3 NIV)

God is telling us we are denser than the animals. We do not know our Master or know His manger. God had brought the Israelites out of slavery in Egypt. He had given them the Promised Land. He had protected them in wars. He had given them life. Israel does not acknowledge Him and understand Him. We have the same problem today.

I came home from work in Richmond in time to go with Henry Gill to feed the cows on the Robinson farm. When we got to a field prior to the Robinson farm, there were the cows grazing in the neighbor's field. There was a patch of woods between the field and the pasture. I thought, *This is going to be fun chasing these cows through the woods and back into the pasture.*

The cows recognized the master's truck that came to feed them and lined up and walked through the woods and into the fence and met us in the barn lot where they were used to being fed. Today, we hear a lot about thinking outside the box. We are encouraged to think outside the box. I challenge you to think inside the box. Our box should be the Word of God and our faith in Jesus Christ. We should know our Master. The cows knew the master's truck. The cows knew where they were fed and came to the location through the woods and through the pasture to the barn lot. We should know our Master, the Lord Jesus Christ, the One who was born in a manger and died on an old rugged cross for our sin. We need to go to the manger to be fed.

Another lesson that I learned from a different group of Gills' cows.

> What do you think? If a man owns a hundred sheep, and one of them wanders away, will he not leave the ninety-nine on the hills and go to look for the one that wandered off?
>
> (Matthew 18:12 NIV)

I have always heard that the grass is greener on the other side of the fence. No matter how good we have it, what the world has to offer seems better than what we have, and more fun. The grass is greener on the other side of the fence, so we think. One night a cow we named Shirley somehow got out of the pasture and wandered down the road. She was seeking greener grass. Shirley was hit by a car. She was lying in a ditch with her tongue hanging out and her legs straight out, knocking on death's door. Henry and Jeannie Gill come upon the scene. Henry loved to eat. He was ready to call a friend who had a wrecker and have him hoist Shirley up and carve Shirley into a side of beef. He was counting the number of steaks he would have. Jeannie loved animals. She had horses and thought of Shirley as a member of the family. Jeannie got down in the ditch and began to pet Shirley and coax her up and helped her back into the pasture. We get out into the world of sin, thinking the grass is greener on the other side of the fence. We are hit by the weight of sin and the world. The devil and the world just see us as a side of beef. Jesus comes to us to pick us up out of the ditch and get us back into His pasture.

> He was oppressed, and he was afflicted, yet he opened not his mouth: he is brought as a lamb to the slaughter, and as a sheep before her shearers is dumb, so he openeth not his mouth.

> (Isaiah 53:7 KJV)

Back in the eighties, we did not have the internet and cell phones to Google questions. I relied on sermon illustration books and Christian reference books in preparing a sermon. When I first went to Shiloh, I used an illustration in a sermon that I thought made a good point. I had read an illustration that sheep have poor eyesight and could only see six-feet at a time. They needed a shepherd because they got lost six feet at a time. We do not intentionally get lost in sin, but we would get lost a little at a time, needing a Savior.

At the end of the sermon, Mr. Carlton Cain challenged me to come and give his ram an eye test. I had never been around sheep. Today, I can Google, "How good is a sheep's eyesight" and get a response of a picture of sheep and an answer. Google says, "Sheep depend heavily on their vision. They have excellent peripheral vision and can see behind themselves without turning their heads. However, they have poor depth perception. They cannot see immediately in front of their noses."[76] Thankfully, I did not try to give Mr. Cain's ram an eye test. I would have gotten head-butted. I did get up early one morning to go to a sheep shearing. I got to see Isaiah 53:7b KJV in person, "The sheep before her shearers was dumb." My Lord and Savior, Jesus Christ, was dumb before His accusers and bore my sins on the old rugged cross.

In 1966, Daddy had a 1952 Dodge pickup and a 1959 Chevrolet car. Neither one was new. The closest way to Stony Creek from Comans Well was through a washboard dirt road. The Dodge pickup was used to haul things for the farm. It had the fenders outside of the

---

[76] "Sheep 101: Sheep Senses." 2014. Sheep 101. 2014. http://www.sheep101.info/senses.html.

bed. Daddy had put helper springs on the pickup to carry the heavy loads. The fender had rusted out because of the fertilizer Daddy had hauled. He had welded the fenders back on with old license plates. I have gone on dates driving the pickup. This was before seat belts. You could not go down the washboard dirt road but so fast because you would bounce all over the seat. You could go down the road at the same speed in the car and feel a little bump but no bouncing all over the seat. What made the difference? Shock absorbers on the car absorbed the shock of the bump. When we put our faith in the Lord Jesus Christ, He absorbs the shocks of life the bumps of life. We Christians have the same trials and temptations in life as anyone, but we are oiled by the Holy Spirit and the love of God through our Savior Jesus Christ.

Why not take the offer?

> I am the door; by me if any man enter in, he shall be saved, and shall go in and out, and find pasture. The thief cometh not, but for to steal, and to kill, and to destroy: I am come that they might have life, and that they might have it more abundantly.

> (John 10:9–10 KJV)

> In my Father's house are many mansions: if it were not so, I would have told you. I go to prepare a place for you. And if I go and prepare a place for you, I will come again, and receive you unto myself; that where I am, there ye may be also.

> (John 14:2–3 KJV)

Jesus offers abundant life and eternal life. Why don't people take the offer of the abundant life here on earth and the promise of a mansion in heaven?

When I first went to work, I was offered to live in an earthly mansion. I drove out to look at the mansion in my Volkswagen Bug.

The house is on the market for almost three and a half million now. It has more bathrooms than we had rooms in our home in Comans Well. At the time, we did not have an indoor bathroom. Recently I visited a church member in the hospital; I road by the mansion and wondered how different my life might have been if I had taken the offer to live there? Why didn't I take the offer? I believe many people turn down Jesus' offer for the same reason I turned down my earthly offer to live in a mansion.

Reason number one was I felt I was not good enough to live in a mansion like that.

> Then said I, Woe is me! For I am undone; because I am a man of unclean lips, and I dwell in the midst of a people of unclean lips: for mine eyes have seen the King, the Lord of Hosts.
>
> (Isaiah 6:5 KJV)

Thankfully, we do not have to be good enough to accept Jesus as our Lord and Savior. God sent a seraphim with a live coal to touch the lips of Isaiah to take away his iniquity. Jesus shed blood on the cross, washes away our iniquity. All we have to do is confess our sins and accept Him.

Reason number two was I did not want to make any changes in my lifestyle. I did not want any responsibility.

> Now the word of the Lord came unto Jonah the son of Amittai, saying, Arise, go to Nineveh, that great city, and cry against it: for their wickedness is come up before me. But Jonah rose up to flee unto Tarshish from the presence of the Lord...
>
> (Jonah 1:1–3 KJV)

We live in a Burger King world where we want to have it our way. We do not want to surrender to the Will of God. I wanted to go to Comans Well for the weekends to be with my family and friends. I did not want responsibilities in my earthly mansion. I believe God has a call for each of our lives, and we need to follow the Holy Spirit's leadership in living out the abundant life.

My third reason was that I couldn't afford it.

For God so loved the world, the He gave His only begotten Son, that whosoever believeth in him should not perish, but have everlasting life.

(John 3:16 KJV)

Salvation is a free gift from God. Thank God at the age of eight, I accepted the offer from God. I am glad I did not turn down my promise of abundant life and a heavenly mansion like I did to live in an earthly mansion.

Thank you for reading the life story of a saved sinner, a squeaking wheel of Comans Well, Virginia. May God Bless!

References

Bodenharmer, Tom. n.d. "The Hopper Brother & Connie TV Favorites." Greenville, SC: Mark Five. Back Cover.

Bradford, William. 1997. *Of Plymouth Plantation 1620-1647.* New York, NY: Alfred A. Knopf.

"Come, Thou Fount of Every Blessing by Robert Robinson, 1758." n.d. Hymnary.Org. 2020. https://hymnary.org/text/come_thou_fount_of_every_blessing.

Cowley, Geoffrey. 2002. "Hepatitis C: The Insidious Spread Of A Killer Virus." Newsweek. https://www.newsweek.com/hepatitis-c-insidious-spread-killer-virus-142921.

Creek Ripplings: Moments To Remember. 1964. Volume XVI. Stony Creek, Virginia: Stony Creek High School.

Davis, Keith F. 2006. *All These Years: The Authorized Biography of the Hoppers.* First Edit. Woodland Press, LLC.

Dowely, Tim. 1978. *Eerdmans' Handbook to the History of Christianity.* Hertz, England: Lion Publishing.

Ethridge, Grant. 2018. "Bible Studies for Life: KJV Adults" 6 (2): 110.

Hatcher, William E. 1943. "Shiloh Still Lives." *The Sunday School Builder*, 1943.

"I Hear You Knocking Written by Dave Bartholomew and Pearl King, 1955." n.d. Lyrics.Com. 2020. https://www.lyrics.com/lyric/16409252/Dave+Edmunds/I+Hear+You+Knocking.

"Isaac Robinson (1610–1704)." 2009. Find A Grave Memorial. 2009. https://www.findagrave.com/memorial/34758126/isaac-robinson.

"Isaac Robinson 1744–1807." 2020. Ancestry. Com. 2020. Ancestry.com/family-tree/person/tree/159990938person/382092415489/story.

"John Robinson (Pastor)." 2020. Wikipedia, The Free Encyclopedia.

2020. https://en.wikipedia.org/wiki/John_Robinson_(pastor).

"John Smyth: English Minister." 2020. In *Encyclopædia Britannica*. Encyclopædia Britannica, inc. https://www.britannica.com/biography/John-Smyth.

Jones, Richard L. 1994. *The History of a Community Bank: The Bank of Southside Virginia, 1905-1991*. Bank of Southside Virginia/Dietz Press. https://www.amazon.com/History-Community-Bank-Southside-1905-1991/dp/0875170765.

No Pulishing Information Available. 1928. "Newspaper Clipping from the Collection of Frances Mayes," 1928.

"Notes on the History of Shiloh Baptist Church: 125th Anniversary, 1975." n.d.

"Personal Notes on Cedar Level during the Civil War by Regina Davis." n.d.

"Quote by Abraham Lincoln." n.d. Quotetab. 2020. https://www.quotetab.com/quote/by-abraham-lincoln/i-am-now-the-most-miserable-man-living-if-what-i-feel-equally-distributed-to-the?source=men.

"Rev John Robinson Jr. (1576–1625) Find A Grave Memorial." 2002. Find A Grave Memorial. 2002. https://www.findagrave.com/memorial/6238808/john-robinson.

"Sappony Baptist Church." n.d. Sappony Baptist Church. 2020. https://www.sappony1773.org/.

"Sappony Indians." n.d. NCPedia: State Library of NC. 2020. https://www.ncpedia.org/sappony-indians.

"Sheep 101: Sheep Senses." 2014. Sheep 101. 2014. http://www.sheep101.info/senses.html.

"Sussex Charge - Petersburg District, Virginia Conference, Sharon United Methodist Church 1850–1975." n.d.

The Holy Bible: King James Version [KJV]. 1999. New York, NY: American Bible Society. Public Domain.

The Holy Bible: New International Version [NIV]. 1984. Grand

Rapids: Zonderman Publishing House. https://www.
biblegateway.com/versions/New-International-Version-NIV-
Bible/#booklist.

"U.S., Appointments of U. S. Postmasters, 1832–1971." 2020.
Ancestry.Com. 2020. https://www.ancestry.com/search/
collections/1932/.

"William H Coleman." 2020. Ancestry.Com. 2020.
William H Coleman,ancestry.com%0Aancestry.
com/familytree/78467263/person/3639059364/
facts?phsrc=mmh640&phstaet=successSource%0A.

"William Robinson 1785–1854." 2020. Ancestry.Com. 2020.
Ancestry.com/family-tree/person/tree/1609777755/
person/392116031581/facts.

Williams, Gary Murdock. 2012. *Sussex County, Virginia: A
Heritage Recalled by the Land.* The Dietz Press.

Writers' Program (U.S.). Virginia, Virginia Writers' Project.
1942. *Sussex County: A Tale of Three Centuries.* Whittet &
Shepperson.

CPSIA information can be obtained
at www.ICGtesting.com
Printed in the USA
BVHW070608240221
600901BV00008B/555